The Use of Performance Indicators in Higher Education

A Critical Analysis of Developing Practice

Second Edition

The Higher Education Policy series

Study Abroad Programmes
Edited by B. Burn, Ladislav Cerych and Alan Smith
*Higher Education Policy Series 11, **Volume I***

Impacts of Study Abroad Programmes on Students and Graduates
Susan Opper, Ulrich Teichler and Jerry Carlson
*Higher Education Policy Series 11, **Volume II***

Major American Higher Education Issues in the 1990s
Richard I Miller
Higher Education Policy Series 9

Academics and Policy Systems
Edited by Thorsten Nybom and Ulf Lundgren
Higher Education Policy Series 8

Governmental Strategies and Innovation in Higher Education
Edited by Frans van Vught
Higher Education Policy Series 7

Changing Patterns of the Higher Education System: The Experience of Three Decades
Ulrich Teichler
Higher Education Policy Series 5

Evaluating Higher Education
Edited by Maurice Kogan
Higher Education Policy Series 6

Higher Education and the Preparation for Work
Chris J. Boys, John Brennan, Mary Henkel, John Kirkland, Maurice Kogan, Penny Youll
Higher Education Policy Series 4

Graduates at Work: Degree Courses and the Labour Market
John Brennan and Philip McGeevor
Higher Education Policy Series 1

Degrees of Success: Career Aspirations and Destinations of College, University and Polytechnic Graduates
Chris J. Boys with John Kirkland
Higher Education Policy Series 2

Higher Education Policy Series 3

The Use of Performance Indicators in Higher Education

A Critical Analysis of Developing Practice

Second Edition

Martin Cave, Stephen Hanney and Maurice Kogan

Jessica Kingsley Publishers
London

First published in the United Kingdom in 1991 by
Jessica Kingsley Publishers Ltd
118 Pentonville Road
London N1 9JN

British Library Cataloguing in Publication Data
The use of performance indicators in higher education: a
critical analysis of developing practice. - (Higher
education policy series: 0954 3716 : 2)
1. Higher education institutions. Efficiency. Assessment
I. Cave, Martin II. Hanney, Stephen III. Kogan, Maurice
IIII. Series
379.154

ISBN 1-85302-518-6

Printed and bound in Great Britain by
Biddles Ltd, Guildford and King's Lynn

Contents

List of Figures and Tables

Preface to the Second Edition

This book is an updated account of the present use and status of performance indicators (PIs) in British higher education. As in the first edition, our descriptions and conclusions are set against the developing literature and experience of PIs in the USA and other countries.

Writing about PIs must be set against the background of major shifts in higher education policy in the UK and in other countries. In the UK over the last seven years, a series of government and central agency reports and policy announcements have altered the landscape of higher education policy. We attempt to give a dispassionate account of the changes so that higher education teachers and researchers, those who administer institutions and systems, and those who are interested in their performance can make informed choices about the uses to which they would put performance indicators. The book thus provides a critical survey of the range of devices now being proposed but also, in its concluding chapter, points to possible patterns or strategies of use.

At the time when we published our first edition, both the general literature on PIs and evaluation and recent UK writing and policy pronouncements largely concerned the universities. Since then, however, material emanating primarily from the Polytechnics and Colleges Funding Council (PCFC) has contributed to the literature of the subject and is incorporated in this present account.

We are grateful to Richard Bell who made a major contribution to our research, especially to Chapter 4. Juliet Poole drafted some of the material in Chapter 3. Several people were kind enough to read the manuscript of the first edition and comment on it - notably Philip Chatwin, Duncan Harris, Richard Miller and John Sizer. We emphasise that the performance of this task in no way implies that they share our views. Gillian Trevett was our co-author in the first edition and we remain grateful for her expert and critical contributions to it.

We also express gratitude to Sally Harris who expertly collated and reproduced contributions from our team and saw both editions to the press.

M. Cave, S. Hanney and M. Kogan
Faculty of Social Sciences
Brunel University, 1991

Chapter 1

Key Issues in the Development of Performance Indicators

1.1 The Policy Background

The introduction of performance indicators into higher education in the UK was the product of a highly political process involving the government, the Committee of Vice-Chancellors and Principals (CVCP) and the then University Grants Committee (UGC).*

On 28 March 1984, the then Education Secretary, Sir Keith Joseph announced that 'in response to my wish that there should be an efficiency study in the universities the Committee of Vice-Chancellors and Principals have proposed, and I have agreed, that the study should be conducted under their aegis'. The CVCP invited Sir Alex Jarratt, an industrialist, former civil servant and Chairman of the Council of Birmingham University to chair the Steering Committee that was to promote and co-ordinate the study. The Jarratt Report (1985) recommended that universities and the system as a whole must work to clear objectives and achieve value for money. It made many other recommendations concerned with the establishment of strong management and planning structures. Among these it proposed the introduction of performance indicators.

On 20 May 1986 Sir Keith Joseph told the House of Commons that the government was to consider with the UGC and CVCP some further financial provision for the universities in 1987/88 and the following years but 'that the government's willingness to make such provision depended crucially on evidence of real progress in implementing and building upon the changes that are needed'. The areas identified were selectivity in the distribution of resources, the rationalisation and, where appropriate, the closure of small departments, better financial management and improved

* Now replaced, under the Education Reform Act, 1988, by the Universities Funding Council.

standards of teaching. Following this announcement, the UGC and CVCP came to accept what is known as the Concordat; if changes in university management as requested by the government were met, further finance would be released to the universities. By November 1986 both Committees were able to make a report of progress to Kenneth Baker, who by then had succeeded Sir Keith Joseph, and among the developments reported was the publication of the first of a Joint Working Party's *Report on the Use of Performance Indicators* relating to both inputs and outputs in teaching and research.

These developments are to be set against the background of a series of reports and policy proposals for performance measurement in the public services in general (Cave et al 1990) that have emanated from central government and its funding agencies over the last few years, a point fully recognised in the recent report from the PCFC (Morris 1990). Since 1981 the government was committed to changes in the funding and national planning of universities, polytechnics and colleges in England. It revised its policy on access to higher education. It accepted the proposals of the Committee under the Chairmanship of Lord Croham (1987) for the replacement of the University Grants Committee by the Universities Funding Council (UFC). It decided to make the UFC responsible for the distribution of funds among universities under new contract arrangements and to establish a new Polytechnics and Colleges Funding Council (PCFC) which has submitted public sector institutions, too, to a system of contract funding. And it made various other proposals, including the introduction of performance indicators, which it believed would lead to greater quality and efficiency in higher education.

The principal reports and policy proposals since 1984 are as follows:

- *1984. University Grants Committee. A Strategy for Higher Education into the 1990s*

Explained new approach to the determination of universities' allocations.

- *1985. UGC Circular Letter 12/85: Planning for the Late 1980s*

Elaborated on principles in UGC Strategy Document. Requested from universities information about their academic and financial plans for the four years ahead.

- *1985. UGC Circular Letter 22/85: Planning for the late 1980s: The Resource Allocation Process*

Letter to universities explaining the new resource allocation procedure. Referred to research performance indicators but stated that 'there are few indicators of teaching performance that would enable a systematic external assessment of teaching quality to be made'. If universities know how to do it 'the Committee would be glad to be told how they have done it'. A suitable methodology for taking account of teaching quality could be used in due course.

- *1985. STEAC Report. Report of the Scottish Tertiary Education Advisory Council. Future Strategy for Higher Education in Scotland, Cmnd 9676.*

Report on the planning and funding of higher education in Scotland. Stated that continued access by the Scottish universities to a UK based peer review system would be desirable.

- *1985. Jarratt Report. CVCP. Report of the Steering Committee for Efficiency Studies in Universities.*

Universities and the system as a whole should work to clear objectives and achieve value for money. Made proposals for the functioning of the DES and the UGC. Recommended that the UGC and CVCP should develop performance indicators. Made recommendations on university policy and management structures, including: strengthening of role of council; rolling academic and institutional plans; Vice-Chancellor to be Chief Executive for the University; small planning and resources committee; budget delegation to appropriate centres; performance indicators; a more streamlined managerial structure.

- *1985. Green Paper. The Development of Higher Education into the 1990s (Cmnd 9524).*

Rejected an 'over-arching' body for higher education. Revoked the concept of deficiency financing to universities (the system whereby universities were allocated funds sufficient to cover their costs), but conceded that for the foreseeable future the main source of income will be the tax payer. Made no definite commitment to future plans for funding and access. Advocated development of PIs.

- *1985. Committee of Vice-Chancellors and Principals. Steering Committee for Efficiency Studies in Universities. National Data Study*

The research study commissioned from consultants and researchers to back up the work of the Jarratt Committee.

- *1985. Lindop Report. Academic Validation in Public Sector Higher Education, Cmnd 9501.*

Made proposals for modes of validation to be adopted in the public sector, including stronger moves towards self- evaluation.

- *1986. UGC Circular Letter 4/86. Planning for the Late 1980s: Recurrent Grant for 1986/87.*

This letter gave details of the basis of the 1986/87 grant allocation and in Part III, Annex 3 published research gradings of universities 'cost centres'.

- *1986. Performance Indicators in Universities: A First Statement, by a joint CVCP/UGC Group.*

Outlined a set of possible performance indicators, capable of realisation over different time horizons.

- *1986. CVCP. Reynolds Report. Academic Standards in the Universities.*

Set up codes of practice on the maintenance and monitoring of standards, including external examining and postgraduate training and research.

- *1987. Croham Report. Review of the University Grants Committee, Cm 81.*

Proposed the reconstitution of the UGC as a university grants council with broadly equal numbers of academic and non-academic members, a non-academic Chairman and a full- time Director General drawn from the academic world. UGC to have 'unambiguous powers to attach conditions to grant'. Other proposals for tightening up accountability of universities.

- *1987. White Paper. Higher Education: Meeting the Challenge, Cm 114.*

Stated aims and purposes of higher education. Student numbers to return to present levels in mid-1990s and then grow again. Age participation rate to increase to 18%. Made recommendations for quality and efficiency including more selectively funded research, 'targeted with attention to prospects for commercial exploitation', and proposed improvements in management of the system. Favoured development and use of performance indicators. Established new Polytechnics and Colleges Funding Council (PCFC) and Universities Funding Council (UFC). Proposed new contract arrangements for both sectors.

- *1987. Clayton Report on The Measurement of Research Expenditure in Higher Education. University of East Anglia.*

Proposed a method for allocating costs between teaching and research and calculated average cost of research output.

- *1987. The Oxburgh Report. Report by E. R. Oxburgh. Strengthening University Earth Sciences. UGC.*

Report on rationalisation of earth sciences from which proposals for grading of institutions on research potential have evolved.

- *1987. ABRC. A Strategy for the Science Base*

Identified a lack of purposeful direction in the deployment of university research effort. Recommended creation of three types of institution (R, T and X) and greater emphasis on programme grants. Emphasis on inter-disciplinary research centres. Criteria for establishing priorities to be internal (timeliness, pervasiveness and excellence) and external (exploitability, applicability and significance for education and training).

- *1987. DES. Changes in Structure and National Planning for Higher Education. Polytechnics and Colleges Sector*

Elaborates the proposal to set up the Polytechnics and Colleges Funding Council.

- *1987. DES. Changes in Structure and National Planning for Higher Education. Universities Funding Council.*

Expands on government's initial response to the Croham Committee's recommendations.

- *1987. DES. Changes in Structure and National Planning for Higher Education. Contracts between the Funding Bodies and Higher Education Institutions.*

Gives details of alternative proposals for system of contracting between institutions and the new planning and funding bodies to replace grants.

- *1987. CVCP and UGC. Second Statement by the CVCP/UGC Working Group*

Lists (with commentary) 39 performance indicators scheduled for publication later in the year.

- *1987. DES. Accounting and Auditing in Higher Education*

Consultative document outlining procedures for improving accounting and auditing, which would give the DES considerable powers of inspection.

- *1987. CVCP and UGC. University Management Statistics and Performance Indicators in the UK.*

Publication of 39 sets of comparative cost data and PIs for British universities.

- *1988. Education Reform Act.*

Created Funding Councils for Universities and Polytechnics and Colleges. Provides for incorporation of non-university institutions.

- *1988. CVCP and UGC. University Management Statistics in the UK.*

Second edition. Includes an increased number of PIs; up from 39 to 54.

- *1989. UFC. Circular Letter 27/89. Research Selectivity Exercise 1989. The Outcome.*

Published the ratings for units of assessment and cost centres following the research selectivity exercise. Ratings to be used to inform calculations of grant.

- *1989. CVCP and UFC. Performance Indicators Steering Committee. Issues in Quantitative Assessment of Departmental Research.*

A consultative document from the Sub-Committee on Research Indicators setting out the issues surrounding the development of research performance indicators.

- *1989. PCFC. Recurrent Funding Methodology 1990/91. Guidance for Institutions.*

Set out the funding method adopted by the PCFC following a consultative exercise on four options. The allocations to consist of two elements: core-funding based on a percentage of the previous year's allocation - 95 per cent in the first year - and an element for which institutions bid competitively.

- *1989. CVCP and UFC. University Management Statistics in the UK*

Third edition. A few of the 54 PIs used in the second edition were slightly amended.

- *1989. Sutherland Report. CVCP. VC/89/160A. The Teaching Function. Quality Assurance.*

Proposals based upon the recommendations of a group chaired by Prof. Stewart Sutherland to create a CVCP academic audit unit to monitor universities' own quality assurance. The unit has since been set up.

- *1989. Kingman Report. CVCP. Costing of Teaching in Universities.*

Report of the work of the group chaired by Sir John Kingman. They concluded that if allowance is made for that research and scholarly activity essential for teaching, almost all the cost of academic staff (except research staff) should be included in the teaching cost.

- *1989. UFC. Circular Letter 39/89. Funding and Planning: 1991/92 to 1994/95.*

Explained how the council intended to determine the distribution of recurrent funds in the four year period from 1991/92. For funding on teaching-based criteria, universities were invited to submit offers of student places. Funding on research-based criteria to be increasingly selective based on the assessments contained in Circular Letter 27/89.

- *1989. UFC. Report on the 1989 Research Assessment Exercise.*

Described the results of the consultative exercise prior to the 1989 exercise and how the ratings were derived in 1989.

- *1990. PCFC. Recurrent Funding and Equipment Allocations for 1990/91.*

The results of the first round of the new funding methodology were announced along with a document, *In Pursuit of Quality: An HMI View*, explaining the inspectorate's approach to quality and context for its advice to the Council's Programme Advisory Groups on claims for 'outstanding quality'.

- *1990. PCFC. Performance Indicators. Report of a Committee of Enquiry Chaired by A. Morris.*

Recommended PCFC publish four sets of 'macro performance indicators' relevant to national aims and objectives to illuminate the 'Public Expenditure Compact' it negotiates with the Government. Institutions should use a corporate planning process designed primarily by the institutions to their own specifications but involving the use of performance indicators. Institutions should publish some of their chosen institutional performance indicators in an annual 'performance report'. The Council should introduce a rolling system of triennial institutional review visits which would, as a final stage in the process of institutional self-evaluation, review with the institution its self-critical appraisal of performance in relation to its mission statement and as illustrated by the institution's chosen performance indicators.

- *1990. PCFC and CNAA. The Measurement of Value Added in Higher Education.*

Report of a joint project to test different approaches to the calculation of the value added achieved by students, based on the comparison of entry and exit qualifications. Recommended the adoption of a comparative value added method which looks at the difference between the actual and expected exit qualifications.

- *1990. PCFC. Teaching Quality. Report of a Committee of Enquiry Chaired by Baroness Warnock.*

Recommended six strategies to the Council designed to enable institutions to demonstrate the quality of their teaching. One strategy is to promote and develop quantifiable and other information relating to the quality of teaching and the report endorsed the finding of the Report on Performance Indicators.

- *1990. CVCP and UFC. University Management Statistics and Performance Indicators in the UK.*

Fourth edition.

- *1990. UFC. Circular Letter 29/90. Funding and Planning Exercise.*

Announced the Council was unable to accept 'the limited scale of economy' offered by the universities' bids over the four year planning period.

- *1990. CNAA. Information Services Discussion Paper 4. Performance Indicators and Quality Assurance.*

Considers the contribution which performance indicators can make to quality assurance. Not a policy statement. Contains a useful categorisation of the various lists of performance indicators proposed in reports produced for universities, polytechnics and colleges.

In our first edition we noted how universities rather than public sector institutions bore the brunt of central authorities' determination that they should display the quality of their performance. In its White Paper (1987), however, the government stated that it would look to the new planning and funding body 'to take the lead in promoting performance indicators in the polytechnics and colleges'. In fact, the public sector had already long had forms of evaluation employed by HMI and CNAA. And before the PCFC got fully to work there had been statements by the Chartered Institute of Public Finance and Accountancy (CIPFA) (1984), the Audit Commission (1985 and 1986), the Further Education Unit (1986), the National Advisory Body for Public Sector Higher Education (NAB) (1987) and the Committee of Directors of Polytechnics (CDP) (1987 - see Wright 1989). Indeed, according to the way in which performance measurement is defined, and the degree of its systematic application, it could and has been argued (for example, Pratt 1989) that performance indicators have long been at work in polytechnics and colleges. Not only in the public sector but throughout higher education the discussion of performance indicators is drawing attention to wide issues of accountability, economy, efficiency and effectiveness and, as we shall see, the PCFC has worked hard to specify and define performance measurement within a wide range of institutional and other contexts.

1.2 Central Control and Institutional Autonomy

In the UK the universities traditionally have been autonomous institutions, despite the fact that their funding from UGC and home tuition fees increased from not much more than 30% in 1939 to 76% in 1980/81 (it subsequently dropped to 67% by 1984/85 and 60% by 1988/89). This autonomy was reflected in the receipt of public money to be used in pursuit of purposes to be agreed with, rather than enforced on, them.

If universities in the UK acting through the UGC were free to negotiate their functions with government, even more were they the custodians of their own performance and standards. They made, and make, their own appointments, and ensure the quality of the degrees by the appointment of their own external examiners. They admit students on their own entrance criteria. But there has always been, even at the high noon of post war autonomy, a form of institutional and subject evaluation. The UGC's main task was to distribute the financial allocations determined by the Government. To do so it made judgements through the use of largely informal evaluations by its expert sub-committees. These were, in effect, peer judgements made on a reputational basis, although framed by analysis of likely student demand for different courses and expectations of the resources to be made available by government.

The Jarratt Committee's (1985) emphasis on the use of performance indicators heralded a major shift in evaluation methods. It recommended explicitly quantitative as well as qualitative judgements. This implied (although it was not made overt) a weakening of trust in subjective peer review. Many of the proposals were associated with a 'greater awareness of costs and more cost charging'. More important, however, they may be interpreted as a shift of assumptions about the governance of institutions. Universities have long been regarded as diarchies in which the power of the collegium, as represented by Senate and the academic autonomy of individual teachers, worked in tandem with the hierarchy embodied in the Vice-Chancellor, Deans and Heads of Departments. The lay element represented by the University Council played a primarily fiduciary and supportive role (Becher and Kogan 1980 and forthcoming 1991). Jarratt proposed that Councils should 'assert their responsibilities in governing *their* institutions' (our italics). Using such terminology of management such as 'strategic plans', 'planning, resource allocation and accountability', the proposal was that the 'corporate process' should be put in place. The Vice-Chancellor should become a chief executive. Given this managerial structure, it was not surprising that indicators should be sought which were calculable and usable by managers.

In 1987, a Committee appointed by the Secretary of State, under Lord Croham, proposed the replacement of the UGC and its academic chairman by a University Grants Council, to be chaired by a layman, probably from industry or commerce, but with a distinguished academic as Director-General. The Government modified the recommendations of the Croham Committee to create instead a Universities Funding Council; the notion of 'grants' was thus put to one side. The Chairman was appointed by the Secretary of State, as was the first holder of the post of Director-General, who was to be an eminent academic. It was to make money available to universities on a contract and monitor performances in accordance with those contracts. It 'will enquire into the extent and quality of teaching and research in the universities and plan for their development . . . publish comparative information . . . keep under review the universities' role in providing teaching and research in accordance with any guidance from the Secretary of State . . .' The government therefore intended that universities should make contractual undertakings about their academic outcomes in return for grants. General objectives should be 'clearly perceived' and both 'the allocation of resources to the universities and their subsequent utilisation should be effectively and efficiently managed', (White Paper 1987.)

The contractual arrangements have been incorporated in a process whereby universities bid for student places in each subject area at prices decided by themselves but influenced by the 'guide price' declared for each area by the UFC. In 1990, at the end of the first bidding round, the Secretary of State expressed disappointment that so few of the bids (7 per cent) were below the guide prices. The guides had already allowed for a substantial reduction in the unit of resource, but in view of the apparent failure of government to support the UFC's guide prices, the bidding system seemed to be in extreme difficulty at the end of 1990. By contrast, the PCFC decided to allocate the bulk of money through core funding, based on a percentage of the previous year's allocation and require the institutions to bid competitively for only a minority element of their funding.

The UK was not alone in making moves towards the stronger management of higher education, although, as will be seen from Chapter 2.3 and 2.4, the use of performance indicators and other objective measures of performance were being construed in some other countries as ways in which institutions could become more free from, rather than more strictly controlled by, the centre. Indeed, within the British context, not all of the changes were of one piece. For example, as they came increasingly under central control, the polytechnics and colleges became corporate bodies independent of local authorities under the provisions of the 1988 Education Reform Act. The growing application of performance indicators to the public sector can, indeed, be linked with the growth of their autonomy.

The Jarratt and Croham proposals were largely accepted. The government also announced its intention of substantial increases in the number of student places in the 1990s to yield an increase in the Age Participation Rate from 14% to figures varying between 20% and 30%. It is plain, however, that the increased numbers are to be supported largely by further cuts in the resources per student.

The government stated that it 'adheres to the Robbins Committee definition of higher education objectives: instruction in skills, the promotion of the general powers of the mind, the advancement of learning, and the transmission of a common culture and common standards of citizenship' ' . . . But above all there is an urgent need . . . for higher education to take increasing account of the economic requirements of the country.' So 'government and its central funding agencies will do all they can to encourage and reward approaches by higher education institutions which bring them closer to the world of business'. This intention was backed up by the award of substantial grants to institutions by the Training Agency to mount projects which would 'embed enterprise into the curriculum'.

The government was thus increasingly determined to ensure that higher education institutions met objectives determined outside themselves, and demonstrate that they had achieved these goals. It is against that background that the development of PIs must be considered.

The indicator movement is in full swing even though the extent to which they were used by the UGC in its 1985 and 1989 rankings remains far from clear. UGC/UFC judgements on research performance are affecting the allocation of funds to individual institutions (see Chapter 4). The Advisory Board for Research Councils suggested ranking universities into three levels according to the amount of research which they will be funded to perform. Stratification is occurring through the differences in monies allowed to universities according to the research gradings of their cost centres rather than through explicit designation.

The use of PIs is a highly political issue. Their use, and the associated use of peer evaluation, can be defined as the generation of judgements about performance (some but not all of which rest on essentially academic evaluations) and their transformation into managerial tools. They are being formally developed as part of an attempt to reorientate the higher education system towards more evaluation in general and more public forms of evaluation in particular.

1.3 Defining Performance Indicators in Higher Education

Despite the growing attention paid to performance indicators for higher education, there is no single authoritative definition or interpretation of their nature.

In the survey carried out under the OECD's Institutional Management in Higher Education (IMHE) Programme, an indicator is defined as 'a numerical value used to measure something which is difficult to quantify'. Thus in the questionnaire sent out under the IMHE Programme, performance indicators were described as 'numerical values which can be derived in different ways. They provide a measurement for assessing the quantitative or qualitative performance of a system. For example, the ratio between output and input (ie benefits obtained and resources consumed) can be an indicator. Indicators need not be so strictly defined, however, and those which relate to quality should also be included for the purposes of this survey' (Cuenin 1986).

Cuenin draws a distinction between simple indicators, performance indicators and general indicators. Simple indicators, he suggests, are usually expressed in the form of absolute figures and are intended to provide a relatively unbiased description of a situation or process. This corresponds roughly to the UGC's use of the term 'management statistics'. Performance indicators differ from simple indicators in that they imply a point of reference, for example a standard, an objective, an assessment, or a comparator, and are therefore relative rather than absolute in character. Although a simple indicator is the more neutral of the two, it may become a performance indicator if a value judgement is involved. In order to avoid possible ambiguity, Cuenin proposes the general rule that performance indicators should have the following property:

> 'when the indicator shows a difference in one direction this means that the situation is better, whereas, if it shows a difference in the opposite direction, then this means that the situation is less favourable. The way in which the data are to be interpreted ought to be obvious.'

There are in addition, Cuenin suggests, very general indicators which in the main are derived from outside the 'institution and are not indicators in the strict sense - they are frequently opinions, survey findings or general statistics'. Although they may not conform exactly to the definition of an indicator they are used in decision making, and he argues, 'these general indicators could be converted into legitimate performance indicators, but it would seem there is no great desire to do so'. It could be maintained, for example, that the peer review exercise carried out by the UGC in 1986 into the quality of research in UK universities was just such an attempt to convert a general indicator into a performance indicator (see Chapter 4.1). The Morris Report advocated that the HMI's database of current inspection reports should be used as an indicator, at sector level, of the proportion of work in each PCFC Programme area, and overall, which falls within each of the five broad quality descriptors used by the HMI.

Others (for example, CIPFA 1984) suggest that indicators are more tentative than measures or findings. Similarly, in 1986 the CVCP/UGC Working Group defined PIs as 'statements, usually quantified, of resources employed and achievements secured in areas relevant to the particular objectives of the enterprise' and went on to suggest that the emphasis is 'on indicators as signals or guides rather than absolute measures' and that whilst indicators do not necessarily provide direct measurements of inputs, processes and outputs, they can offer valuable information relating to them. More recently the concept of PIs has been widened to embrace management statistics; these are normally comparative data, typically relating to costs, which can be used for management and control functions but which do not pretend to assess performance in a comprehensive sense. Thus the compilation of data published by the UGC in 1987 was called *Management Statistics and Performance Indicators.*

Another property claimed for performance indicators is that 'they reduce a complexity of subjective judgements to a single objective measure' (Laurillard 1980). She questions the validity of such an approach, but the point about reducing complexity is also made by Frackmann (1987) who concludes that 'performance indicators stand for simplified information that is needed for management and organisation. Performance indicators are always to be used by outside or higher levels of decision making, compared with the performing unit under review.'

Different Categories of Performance Indicators

There are a variety of intersecting attempts to categorise performance indicators. The *Jarratt Report* (1985) distinguished between 'internal', 'external' and 'operating' indicators. The first category includes variables which have the common features of reflecting either inputs into the institution (attractiveness of undergraduate or graduate courses, attraction of research funds) or valuations internal to the institution (award of degrees, teaching quality). External indicators reflect the valuations of an institution in the 'market place' of its subjects - the employment of its graduates or acceptance of its publications. Operating performance indicators include 'productivity' ratios such as unit costs and reflect variables such as workloads or availability of library stocks or computing facilities.

The *1986 Report of the CVCP/UGC Working Party* distinguished the more conventional categories of input, process and output performance indicators. Input indicators have to do with the resources, human and financial, employed by universities. Process indicators relate to the intensity or productivity of resource use and to the management effort applied to the inputs and to the operation of the organisation. Output indicators are about what has been achieved; the products of the institution.

This categorisation implies acceptance of the applicability of the 'production model' to universities - the notion (set out more fully in the following section) that concepts borrowed from industrial management have a role in the university sector. By implication, this model suggests acceptance not only of input, process and output variables but also of uncontrollable background or environmental variables. These are not as significant in higher education as in other levels of education, but to some extent the physical endowment of educational institutions (including their location) will not be capable of much modification in the short-to-medium term, and the ability of students can reasonably be regarded as uncontrollable in comparisons between sectors of higher education.

Given the array of input, process, output and background variables how, Cullen (1987) asks: 'can they be assembled in performance indicators?' He suggests that a conventional categorisation based on management concepts would distinguish three types of indicators - indicators of efficiency, of effectiveness, and of economy. These conventionally relate to inputs and outputs only. Background variables can be entered as if they were inputs, providing that prior analysis has indicated how they should be expected to relate to outputs. He suggests that 'process variables may be of interest in explaining the values found for the performance indicators, but they cannot themselves be used directly as performance indicators'. Attention is currently being given to ways of incorporating evaluation of processes into performance indicators. Indicators of economy are conventionally defined as those which compare actual with target inputs' and thus measure input savings; indicators of efficiency are those which compare outputs with inputs - normally actual outputs with actual inputs. Effectiveness indicators show whether the objectives of policy have been achieved.

As an illustration of this distinction, the 1987 White Paper, in supporting the use of performance indicators, noted that the CVCP/UGC 1986 list covered both efficiency indicators including: 'student-staff ratios (SSRs) and a range of unit costs broken down by the main categories of expenditure'; and effectiveness indicators including: 'income from research grants and contracts, the number of research and sponsored students, submission rates for research degrees, the first occupation of graduates and the institution's contribution to postgraduate and professional training'. Moreover, 'unit costs and SSRs are now accepted indicators of the intensity of resource use'.

The PCFC's definition (Morris 1990) is: 'Performance indicators are statistics, ratios, costs and other forms of information which illuminate or measure progress in achieving the mission and the corresponding aims and objectives of the PCFC or of a college or polytechnic which it funds.'(paragraph 1.4)

Bringing these definitions and interpretations together, we define a performance indicator as an authoritative measure - usually in quantitative form - of an attribute of the activity of a higher education institution. The measure may be either ordinal or cardinal, absolute or comparative. It thus includes both the mechanical applications of formulae (where the latter are imbued with value or interpretative judgements) and such informal and subjective procedures as peer evaluations or reputational rankings.

This discussion of alternative definitions and categorisations of performance indicators has demonstrated the various interpretations of the term. Throughout we have adopted a broad rather than a narrow definition. But before discussing the various modes in which PIs are applied it is useful to set them within the context of a more familiar model of evaluation.

1.4 Performance Indicators and the Measurement of Inputs and Outputs in Education

Higher education is not unusual in experiencing pressure to measure and appraise performance, and over the last seven or eight years the use of performance indicators has become widespread in public services. Their use within wider evaluative frameworks is discussed in Chapter 5. It is, however, useful to locate performance indicators in relation to other more traditional techniques for economic measurement or evaluation applied over the range of public institutions (Barrow 1990). For higher education this can be achieved by reference to a simplified conceptual framework which views higher education as a process which transforms inputs into outputs, and is itself part of a wider economic and social process.

Figure I illustrates this framework. Higher education is seen as a process for transforming inputs (notably of students' time, academics' time, consumables and equipment and buildings) into outputs which can be broadly classified as relating to either teaching or research. The former includes the value-added of all those receiving instruction from the university or other higher education institutions - undergraduate students,

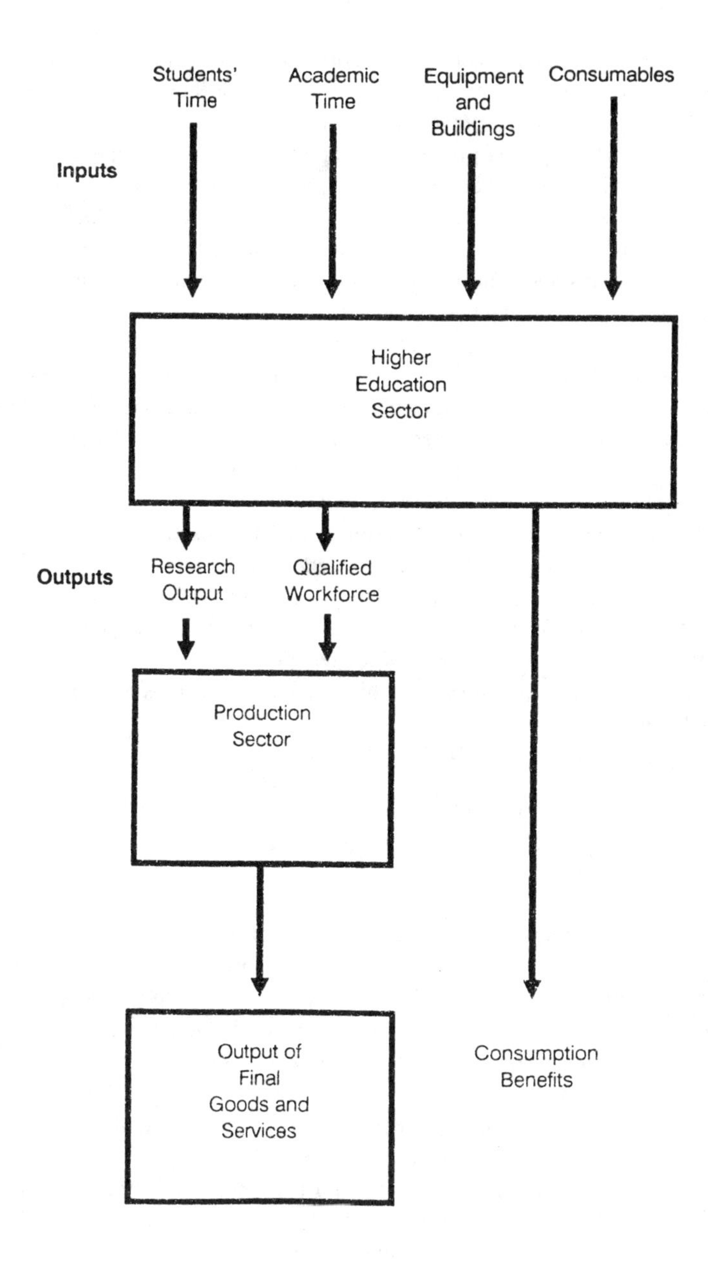

Figure 1. Inputs and Outputs in Higher Education

graduate students and those taking short courses. It includes any increment in the knowledge of students, whether or not they complete their studies. Research is a shorthand for any increase in knowledge generated by the institution, in the form of publications, patents, development work, and the like. Many university activities, notably the preparation of research degrees, combine 'teaching' and 'research' as joint products.

Some higher education outputs are used directly as consumption benefits. For instance, mastery of a discipline or completion of research may yield direct satisfaction. Others are intermediate inputs into other economic processes, or inputs which go back into higher education itself (for simplicity, this feedback is not shown in the diagram). Thus both trained personnel and the results of research are used in all sectors of the economy, including the higher education sector. They are inputs into further transformation processes which generate other outputs, often in the form of consumption goods and services.

Historically, a number of techniques have been used to appraise the efficiency of the higher education process. Typically they involve establishing some relationship between inputs and outputs. Where they differ is in the stage at which inputs and outputs are measured, the units in which they are measured, and the level of aggregation.

The figure thus identifies four points at which measures or indicators can be recorded:

(a) inputs;

(b) process or productivity;

(c) intermediate outputs;

(d) final outputs.

In many commercial activities, flows at all of these points would be measurable in money terms, and the measures ultimately be derived from the valuations of output made by final consumers. But this approach is not possible within higher education as many of the outputs are difficult or impossible to measure in monetary or even in physical units. Hence the emergence of PIs as partial and approximate 'surrogate' measures either of output or - in many cases - of inputs. But it is useful to review other techniques of measurement.

Cost-benefit analysis is one of the most ambitious techniques which has been applied. It has been used to establish the rate of return to investment in higher education either for the economy as a whole (the social return) or for the individual student. In the former case the 'costs' are established by aggregating the teaching-related costs shown in Figure

1. Benefits are normally estimated as the discounted value of the increments in earnings associated with higher education, though it is difficult to separate these from other background or environmental effects. On fairly stringent assumptions about the operation of labour markets, they equal the increments in the individual's marginal product of labour. The calculation thus derives an output valuation from the operation of the economy as a whole. Studies of this kind (for example, Clark and Tarsh 1987) typically distinguish between different disciplines or groups of disciplines (for example, social sciences or engineering) and between different levels of degree (for example, undergraduate degrees or post-graduate degrees). It is not, however, normally possible to distinguish between different institutions of higher education, because of problems of sample size. A similar approach is possible in principle in relation to research outputs, but the difficulties of establishing the economic benefits associated with research products rule it out in practice. Calculation of the returns to higher education have been made for a number of countries as summarised in Psacharopoulos (1985).

A less ambitious technique is cost-effectiveness analysis. Inputs are measured in money terms and outputs in physical units (for example, number of graduates, number of research papers). The key difficulty here is ensuring that the physical unit adequately conveys the attributes of the output. When a homogeneous product is being produced, that assumption is reasonable. But the outputs of higher education differ substantially in quality. With cost-benefit analysis this is captured, in principle at least, by the increment in the market wage of graduates. In cost-effectiveness analysis this is not attempted, and the output measure is typically simply the number of students graduated.

Cost-effectiveness analysis is a particular type of productivity measure, in which inputs are denominated in cost terms and outputs in some physical unit. Alternative output and input measures can also be combined to produce partial productivity measures - for example, output of graduates per member of academic staff (or, more conventionally, students undergoing tuition per member of academic staff - the staff-student ratio). In this instance both output and input are measured in physical units and there is no attempt to control for either the quality of output or the cost or quality of inputs. Such measures do however have the merit that they can be computed fairly quickly and on a disaggregated basis - for example, department by department in any given institution or across departments in the same discipline.

Measures of this kind are a form of performance indicator - although in some treatments this term is reserved for cases where the evaluation does not pretend precisely to capture or measure the true variable which is sought. In other accounts, including the present one, the term is used more widely to convey a range of more or less precise measurements of outputs, inputs, productivity and other features of the process.

As noted above, the use of performance indicators within the non-marketed public sector has expanded significantly in recent years, as part of a central government programme to improve the planning, monitoring and evaluation of performance - to develop as far as possible analogues for the revenue and cost figures available in the sectors. As an illustration of this expansion at the level of central government, the 1987 Public Expenditure White Paper (Treasury) contained about 1,800 output and performance measures, compared with 1,200 in 1986 and 500 in 1985. These include such indicators as the number of hospital in-patient and day cases treated, and the proportion of Ministry of Defence contracts subject to competitive tender. Higher education performance indicators listed in the 1987 White Paper included an index of unit costs in local authority higher education.

Both cost-benefit and cost effectiveness analysis rely upon the assumption that particular costs incurred within higher education institutions can be associated with particular returns. For example, the cost-benefit study cited above (Clark and Tarsh 1987) assumed, in calculating the rate of return to society from undergraduate degrees, that alternatively 67%, 80% or 100% of university costs were associated with teaching, the remainder with research.

The distinction between research and teaching inputs and outputs raises a number of serious difficulties. On the output side, some products such as research degrees represent both teaching and research outputs. On the input side, many costs, in the form of academics' time, central services such as libraries and computer centres, and premises and equipment, are joint or common to both teaching and research.

In 1985 the Department of Education and Science commissioned a study into the allocation of costs between teaching and research, published as Clayton (1987). The author asked a stratified sample of departments and central services in higher education institutions to complete a questionnaire allocating costs as far as possible between teaching and research. The results demonstrated a much higher proportion of expenditure on research in universities than in polytechnics; it was also shown that the proportion of UGC funds devoted to research in universities varied from subject group to subject group - from 50% in physical and biological sciences, to 31% in languages and other arts. In addition, of course, research expenditure financed from sources other than the UGC can be expected to differ among subject groups.

Although these results are plausible, there are still doubts about the methodology employed. This was left largely to the respondents' discretion, and difficulties arose in a number of areas. In particular, it was found difficult to allocate staff time between teaching and research. Where library resources are concerned, it was difficult or impossible to categorise expenditure on books and journals used by students and by lecturers, both to prepare their lectures and do their research. More recently, the question has been re-examined for the Committee of Vice-Chancellors and Principals by a committee under Sir John Kingman which doubted whether 'any analysis of time spent on different academic activities will ever provide useful results'. A different approach was therefore tested and the conclusion reached that if allowance is made for that research and scholarly activity essential for teaching then almost all the cost of academic staff (except of course research staff) should be included in the teaching cost (CVCP/VC/89 161(a)).

This problem is not confined to higher education or to the public sector. It arises, for instance, in the allocation of any joint or common costs among the products of a multi-output firm. Broadly speaking there are two approaches to solving it. One uses available or specially prepared accounting data based on the existing process to make an allocation. The problem here is that the results depend upon the particular conventions adopted, none of which can be shown to be correct. The second approach is to seek to establish the 'stand-alone' cost of each activity separately, and to compare those costs with the combined cost of both activities performed together. The combined cost will often be less than the sum of the individual 'stand-alone' costs, and the latter may have to be scaled down using some convention to produce a final cost allocation.

Within the public utilities field (gas, telecommunications, etc.) the second approach is gaining ground, because it is perceived as being less arbitrary than the first (see Brown and Sibley 1986). But there are obvious difficulties in applying it to higher education institutions, where output profiles and levels of efficiency differ considerably. Cost allocation remains one of the major unresolved problems in establishing performance indicators for higher education.

There is an alternative method for comparing inputs and outputs across a range of higher education institutions, known as the 'efficiency frontier' approach or data envelopment analysis. Unlike cost-benefit analysis, which is capable in principle of establishing whether an activity should be undertaken, the efficiency frontier is only capable of identifying the

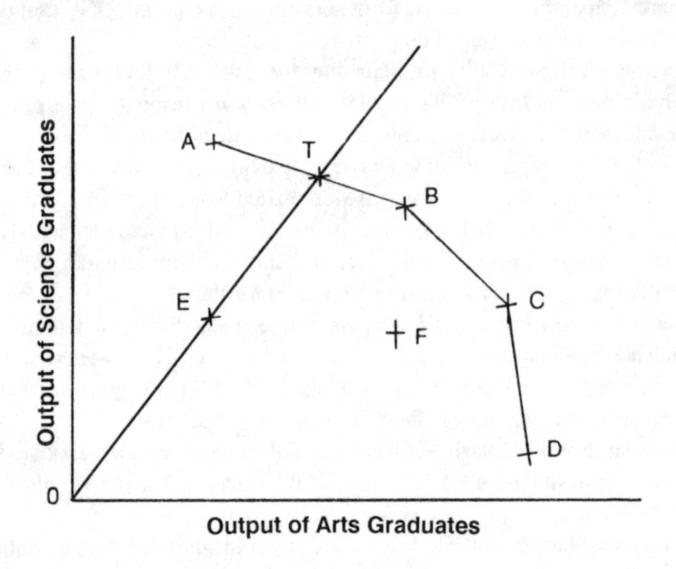

Figure 2. The Efficiency Frontier

most efficient method of doing it, and of showing how close to efficiency a particular institution comes.

As an illustration, suppose that a number of institutions of equal size (and cost) are producing two outputs only, 'arts' and 'science' graduates. Figure 2 shows the outputs of respectively institutions A to F. The 'efficiency frontier' is shown by line ABCD. On the assumption that an institution could be constructed which combines A and B in any given proportions, all points along the chord AB are possible. Similarly, combinations of B and C and of C and D would make possible any points on B C and C D respectively. It would not, however, be efficient to combine, for example, B and D, because the outputs made available could always be produced more efficiently by a combination of B and C or C and D.

In the figure institutions E and F are inefficient, and their degree of inefficiency in the case of E can be measured as the ratio of E T to O T. This shows how much output has been lost as a result of failure to use 'best practice' technology - in this case a combination of those employed by institutions A and B.

The example in Figure 2 is a trivial one as it involves only two outputs and assumes uniform costs across institutions, measured in money terms.

However, the model can be realised (though not, of course, drawn) in as many dimensions as are wanted. Different types of teaching outputs and of research outputs can be distinguished. Costs can be treated as 'negative' or 'inverse' outputs and disaggregated to any desired degree, by department and/or by type - for example, premises, equipment or lecturers' time. There is, however, a trade-off here, in the sense that the greater the degree of disaggregation, the less inefficient any institutions will appear to be as its idiosyncratic cost or output profile promotes it to a point on the frontier.

Hitherto, little use has been made of this technique in higher education, despite its theoretical attractions and its widespread use in other areas of economic analysis. Sizer (1981) reported a single application and expresses doubt about its usefulness. Work has continued, however, aided by the availability of more consistent data (see Tomkins and Green 1988; Ahn et al 1988; and Johnes and Johnes 1990). But its main role, like that of cost-benefit analysis, is to provide a conceptual framework.

The final technique for evaluating performance discussed here is regression analysis. This technique has been used particularly by a group of researchers at Lancaster University - G. Johnes, J. Johnes and J. Taylor. Their detailed findings are described in the chapters which follow, and many are collected in J. Johnes and Taylor (1990). But it is useful here to give a brief account of the principles underlying the technique. This is done on the basis of discussion of a hypothetical performance indicator - research output per staff member.

Suppose that data are available on research output per staff member in a number of university or polytechnic departments within the same discipline. Suppose also that the size of each department is known. The data can then be represented as in Figure 3, where each point shown represents an observation of research output per staff member in a department of the indicated size. The average level for all departments is shown by the horizontal line in the figure. We may formulate the hypothesis that there are features of the production process for research which imply that larger departments produce more research per staff member. This hypothesis can be tested by fitting a line, using standard techniques of statistical regression, through the points in the figure. This line is shown by RR. The closer the fit of points to the line, the greater the proportion of variation in research output per staff member 'explained' by size. But it is highly unlikely that the fit will be perfect. Other factors than size will influence research output per capita; examples are the availability of research funding and equipment, the time and effort devoted to research, and purely random factors.

How can regression analysis be used to improve or refine performance indicators? Given the data at our disposal, the simplest approach would involve comparing each department with the average. On this basis department A would be below average and department B above average. But we may wish to 'correct' our measure of research output per staff member for the size of department. On this basis, department A will have performed better than expected, while department B will have performed worse than expected. Running the regression of research output per staff member on size has enabled us to identify departures above and below the expected output level for a department of any given size.

Regression analysis thus offers two advantages. It makes it possible to test hypotheses concerning factors which affect the production process in higher education. Second, it provides a more refined basis for evaluating the performance of an individual department by comparing the actual outputs with the expected outputs for a given level of inputs. However, it is important to avoid drawing the wrong policy conclusions from the second approach. In Figure 3, A's performance is better than expected and B's worse. In certain circumstances we might be prepared to describe A's behaviour as praiseworthy and B's as blameworthy. But it still remains true that department B has a higher research output per staff member than department A. If the purpose of performance measurement in higher education is not so much to reward and blame but to achieve an efficient allocation of resources, then the (hypothetical) lesson that large departments have a higher research output per staff member is the more significant one.

Despite its apparently reductionist nature, and criticisms, for example by Elton (1988), the production model approach is useful not only for shedding light on particular techniques, but also in illustrating the classification of PIs. The issues surrounding the various classifications of PIs in general are well discussed in Beeton (1988) and with particular reference to higher education, many of these points are brought together in the sequence developed by Sizer (1989) - see Figure 4. The Figure also illustrates the interactive relationship between objectives, measurement and indicators of economy, efficiency, and effectiveness.

The discussion in this section has focussed on the broader conceptual underpinning of performance indicators, and involves much aggregation of variables. Yet within a particular sector and a particular institution there is scope for much more detailed indicators, and for comparison of indicators across institutions. Examples of this kind are considered in subsequent chapters. Nonetheless, when a system of PIs is being devised a proper framework for analysis will help reduce dangers. Mayston

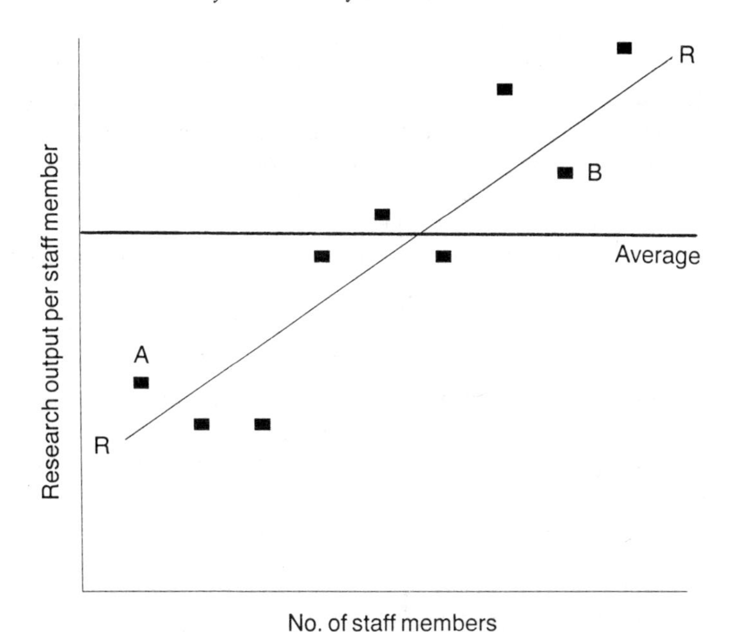

Figure 3. Regression Analysis in a Hypothetical Example

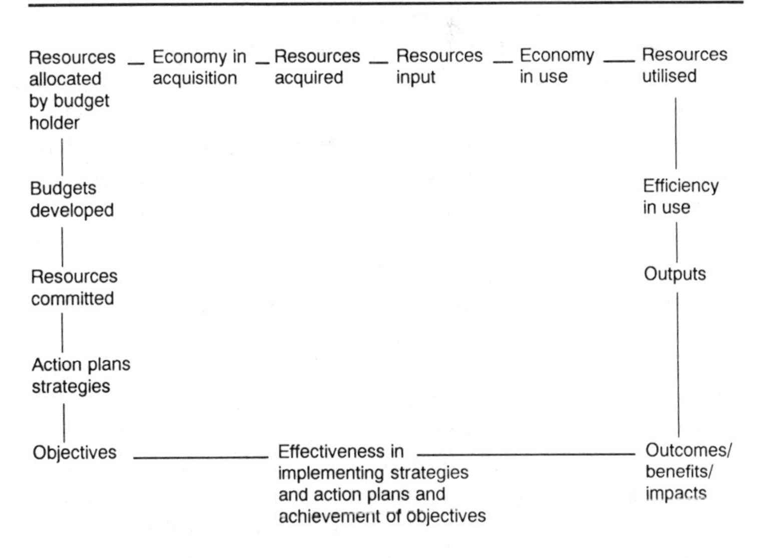

Figure 4. Value for Money - The 3 Es (Source: Sizer 1989)

(1985) showed, on the basis of early American experience, that if PIs lack 'decision relevance' they are ignored. Alternatively, the introduction of PIs may have an impact but a dysfunctional one. It could lead to less easily measured activities being given lower priority and it may affect in unanticipated ways the pattern of working relationships between decision making units and individuals within the organisation, relationships with clients and sponsor, the responsiveness of an organisation to the demands made upon it, and the scope for discretion in the use of resources.

Within the field of higher education and research these dangers can be illustrated by a number of examples:

(a) the greater emphasis being given in universities to research, where PIs already operate, than to teaching (Harris, M. 1986);

(b) a change in the pattern of publications (Cabinet Office 1989);

(c) the greater pressure to publish, irrespective of the state of the material;

(d) the greater emphasis given to types of research where performance can be measured bibliometrically, at the expense of other objectives.

Two further dangers can be noted. First, the partial nature of most indicators leaves ample scope for strategic behaviour on the part of the unit being appraised. This fact has been widely recognised in other contexts: for example in the health service, where use of such indicators as average length of stay of hospital patients is widely believed to have a distorting influence on the pattern of treatment. Clearly similar opportunities exist in higher education, where departments or institutions have considerable scope for determining their input and output mix, and where in many cases members of the institutions themselves largely determine the 'quality' of their output by determining students' degree classes or the completion rate of research degrees - however assiduous external examiners and accrediting bodies may be.

Secondly, there are obvious difficulties in using performance indicators as an input into the resource allocation process. Because of their partial nature, individual performance indicators often provide potentially misleading impressions even of average productivity. For example, two departments may appear to have an equal output of publications per staff member, while one may have a substantially greater amount of complementary inputs. Equally important, resources should be allocated so that contributions of resources are equalised at the margin. The fact that one department may have a lower average level of performance than another does not imply that resources should be taken from the poor performer and given to the good performer. Unless we know about the two departments' relative ability to convert inputs into outputs at the margin, we can make no such claim. Thus the problem of interpretation and use of performance indicators is quite as complex as that of measurement itself. These points are recognised on all sides, not least in the CVCP/UGC documents on performance indicators. It is important, however, that the qualifications are not simply recorded and then ignored, as in the words of Bud (1985), 'disappearing caveats'.

A way of reducing the dangers is not only to develop a framework showing the production function represented by PIs, but also a frame for assessment. Moravcsik (1986) has usefully proposed a 'methodology for finding a methodology' for the assessment of science, though its potential sphere of application is wider. The framework includes:

(a) identifying the relevant objectives of the organisation;

(b) specifying the parts or levels of the system to be analysed and specifying the uses to which the assessment will be put;

(c) listing the PIs to be used;

(d) devising simple strategies for their application to the organisation and predicting the implications that their application might have.

1.5 Plan of the Book

In this chapter we have sought to explore, in general terms, some of the key issues in the development of performance indicators. We have noted how the Government has radically changed the assumptions upon which higher education is to be conducted, and that the introduction of performance indicators forms part of a general shift from academic control over objectives and evaluation to control by the system and its managers. We have briefly enumerated the different definitions and categories of performance indicators, and have related them to the measurement of inputs and outputs in education.

These themes are taken up in Chapter 2 through an overview of recent experience in the United Kingdom, the USA and other countries. Chapters 3 and 4 attempt a closer and more technical survey of the components of performance indicators of both teaching and research. For the most part these chapters rely upon surveys of research undertaken elsewhere.

It will be clear that our approach relies heavily on the distinction between research and teaching outputs and thus implicitly on a division of research-related and teaching-related costs, although we recognise that this involves serious difficulties. We would have liked to include a section on performance indicators in administration, but were prevented from doing so (except inasmuch as the whole PI approach is administrative) by the absence of sufficient literature or experience in higher education of the kind applied, with many limitations, to other areas (for example, Daffern and Walshe 1990).

In Chapter 5 we put some of our descriptions and conceptualisations to work by reflecting on the different models of performance indicators and their modes of application. We thus move from analysis of what is now being proposed in different systems to our own proposals of how they might be used within the United Kingdom context, both by funding bodies and within institutions.

Chapter 2

An Overview of Recent Experiences and Current Perspectives

2.1 Great Britain

Although some performance indicators have always been used in higher education they have been unsystematically applied and their systematic use has been perceived as a threat to the traditional and highly valued autonomy of the institution, the department and the individual. This is partly because the application of PIs, or at least their proper use when policy decisions are being made, depends, it is widely claimed, on the establishment of agreed objectives for higher education. Whilst there are philosophical objections to the concept of objectives-led higher education, without them the successful implementation of PIs is doubtful:

> 'performance indicators are only useful if clear priorities have already been established. Sadly there are no such priorities in higher education policy today. So PIs may be misused' (*Times Higher Education Supplement*, 20 February 1987).

As recently as 1985, the Jarratt Report made it clear that 'objectives and aims in universities are defined only in very broad terms'. The development of objectives for a non-profit making sector such as higher education is immensely difficult. Bourke (1986) claims that:

> 'One notable feature of recent British experience . . . is the absence of specification of goals for single institutions and for the higher education system as a whole. It is a serious problem for British higher education that there is now pressure for quality controls and for evaluation but no agreed statement of system-wide or institutional objectives'.

These factors help explain 'the lack of the systematic use of PIs' (Jarratt). Practical difficulties will be elaborated in later sections but Sizer (1979) had already indicated the complexity of the task several years earlier when he argued that some institutions may be characterised by 'goal conflict rather than by striving towards goal congruence. They have joint inputs and multiple outputs and outcomes, the ultimate impact of which is extremely hard to measure'.

The very nature of higher education is such that it does not allow for measurable and compartmentalised judgements. In referring to Non Advanced Further Education, the Chartered Institute of Public Finance and Accountancy (CIPFA) (1984) thought that genuine complexities made simple indicators seem impracticable. Although some PIs have been introduced and the International Management in Higher Education (IMHE) Programme has given considerable thought to PIs, their study found that the prevailing attitude towards the usefulness of the indicators 'is one of scepticism' (Cuenin 1986).

Frackmann (1987) maintains that those concerned with PI projects may face 'reluctance and strategies of hindrance'. When there is a failure of a PI attempt he suggests it shows that the 'need to change the prevailing situation is not felt thoroughly on both sides of the countervailing powers'.

Despite the scepticism voiced in many academic quarters, the pressures for change from the government and some institutional leaders in higher education in the UK have been considerable and PIs have perforce acquired a higher profile.

The Pressures for Change

Education standards and costs have, of course, been continuously and increasingly under scrutiny since the 'Great Debate' on education from 1976 onwards. At that time institutions of higher education, like other non-profit making organisations, were increasingly being asked to justify their activities and account for their use of resources and their performance to external funding bodies in terms of their efficiency and effectiveness (Sizer 1979). Attempts in the 1970s to apply non-profit performance evaluation techniques, such as programme planning budgeting systems (PPBS) and cost benefit analysis, to the institutions of higher education were not found to be feasible because of their complexity. Nevertheless, Sizer (1979) argued, it might be possible to build on the legacy of PPBS in the development of PIs for the various activities that take place within institutions rather than at the level of the system of higher education.

He further argued that, 'while it may not prove possible to agree objectives, measure outcomes and develop performance indicators for an institution as a whole, it should be possible to do so for parts of the organisation'. Sizer suggested that a whole range of PIs should be considered when establishing indicators for research, teaching and central services and that the following standards should be applied to these partial PIs: relevance, verifiability, freedom from bias, and quantifiability. These standards reappear in the CVCP/UGC working group statement, although Pollitt (1987) has described such lists as being 'next to useless' because they describe 'a state of grace repeatedly envisioned in the managerial scriptures but unknown in the untidy reality'. Whilst this warning is useful, it remains a fact that PIs are being introduced and it is of value to have these standards against which to test them.

The pioneering role of John Sizer in the development of PIs included acting as an adviser when the IMHE Programme also turned its attention to PIs at about the same time (Sizer 1990). It did so because of both the financial constraints being imposed on higher education systems and the other pressures for their application considered here. Despite this and the work of Sizer, when the Society for Research into Higher Education (SRHE) asked in 1979 for papers on PIs they were 'disappointed by the dearth of contributions at institutional and, in particular, at national level' (Billing 1980). Jarratt reported in 1985 that some PIs were used, that a great deal of information was collected by universities and listed some of the indicators used. The Report divided them into the three categories commonly used: internal, external and operational. The apparent contradiction between the reports in 1985 of there being much information collected and the dearth of interest in 1979 can be explained. First, Jarratt reported that much of the information was used for 'administration and not for management', and that there was a lack of systematic use of PIs. Secondly, as Bourke pointed out, the PIs being pursued in the UK,

> 'derive ultimately from the crisis of 1981 and from the need to preserve standards in the face of declining real resources . . . and following the UGC's realisation of the difficulties associated with the application of quality/performance judgements that are confidential and unspecified'.

In 1981 the information that was thought to have influenced the UGC included the amount of income universities received from research councils and the quality of the students on entry. Considerable debate about quality followed the 1981 decisions and the *Times Higher Educational Supplement*, in the absence of any tradition of research in the area, launched a controversial series of surveys of the reputational standing of various departments in British universities.

Accountability continued to be the major topic under discussion throughout the 1980s. In its Green Paper (1985), *The Development of Higher Education into the 1990s*, the government made it clear that it saw the development of performance indicators as the key to value for money. It is perhaps worth quoting at length:

> 'The essential purposes of performance measurement in education are to introduce into considerations of policy and the management of the education system at national and institutional level some concrete information on the extent to which the benefits expected from education expenditure are actually secured, and to facilitate comparisons in terms of effectiveness and efficiency as between various parts of the system, and as between different points in time. The pursuit of value for money in higher education can only be successful if it is based on an analysis of benefits and their related costs in different activities. There are significant difficulties in measuring performance in higher education . . . But the effort has to be made if the government is to pursue its objectives of controlling public expenditure and of making the most effective use of the tax payer's money; and if institutions and others concerned with higher education planning are to be fully informed in taking their decisions on the allocation of the resources available.'

It is clear that the themes of financial constraint and value for money were, and still are, strongly linked because, by devising ways of showing that it is providing value for money, higher education increases its chances of maximising the money allocated to it and, as Jarratt had argued, 'the search for value for money is desirable at any time; in an era of constrained funding it becomes essential'. As noted in Chapter 1, Sizer (1989) set out how the Thatcher Government's demand for greater accountability and value for money in performance in terms of economy, efficiency and effectiveness could be modelled. There was a requirement, as elaborated in the Jarratt Report, for the development of strategic plans to underpin academic decisions and structures, which brought planning, resource allocation and accountability together into a corporate process linking academic, financial and physical aspects.

Jarratt accepted that PIs for universities had proved difficult to devise and that there was no universally accepted series in general use but advocated that a range of PIs should be developed.

In the 1985 Green Paper the DES not only welcomed the Jarratt Report's suggestions for the use of PIs at institutional level, but also discussed their application for evaluating the national system of higher education. It saw the three main outputs of higher education as being highly qualified manpower, research, and other social benefits; it discussed some of the performance measures developed for these outputs but noted that at the national level significant progress was limited to research. Even if the difficulties of constructing these measures could be overcome, there would still be no adjustment for quality of output and no satisfactory measure of a major output of higher education - the impact of highly qualified labour in the economy. The Green Paper suggested that some aspects of these variables could be captured by indicators such as wastage rates, entry standards and graduates' first destinations. The PIs discussed included: student numbers and participation rates; unit costs; recurrent costs; the number and costs of successful students. One measure which, according to the Green Paper, attempts to conflate some of the indicators into an overall index of value for money is the 'rate of return' of higher education. The 'rate of return' is the annual flow of benefits, such as contribution to the economy, which are reflected in higher earnings, expressed as a percentage of the initial cost of education. The Green Paper Annex could be criticised for slipping from a consideration of performance measure at the institutional and national levels to a concentration on the national level only.

Mainly as a result of the Jarratt Report and of government concern about the preservation of academic quality the Committee of Vice-Chancellors and Principals (CVCP) established a Committee under Professor Philip Reynolds (1986) which listed the data that might be, and in many cases already were being, collected by universities and which could be used to monitor academic standards. Many of the points were incorporated in the CVCP/UGC 1986 list of proposed performance indicators. Additionally the DES put considerable effort into the development of PIs to measure the extent to which higher education was serving the needs of the economy for highly qualified manpower (Cullen 1987).

The increasing concern with the interests of the consumer rather than those of the professional producer was not a completely new factor. Particular emphasis, however, is now being given to a broader definition of 'consumer' to include groups such as employers (in, for example, the *Research Into Sandwich Education Report* 1985) in addition to the previous implicit emphasis on students. The attention being given to the development of PIs in several fields, especially the assessment of teaching and first destination studies, may be related to these pressures.

The University Grants Committee likewise had to be actively involved in judgements of quality (Harris, M. 1986). Sir Keith Joseph, when Secretary of State had, in fact, threatened to remove research funding from the UGC to the research councils unless the UGC launched a selectivity exercise. Better evaluation of the quality of existing research has also become more necessary as reduced funding has limited the proportion of 'alpha' quality research proposals that can be supported.

Even in an era of 'steady state' funding, the unparalleled growth in scientific opportunities and ever more expensive equipment means that emphasis is placed on the search for more 'objective' decision aids, rather than relying solely on peer review because the research funding decisions become inevitably more controversial (Gibbons and Georghiou 1987; Ziman 1987; Phillips and Turney 1988). Irvine (1989) suggests that the UK was the first to experience these research pressures. Although such pressures impinged particularly on the research councils they had an impact on higher education.

Generally, at a time of financial restrictions the pressures on the funding bodies - both at national level and within the institutions - to justify how they reach their decisions become greater. The lack of debate about, or announcement of, explicit criteria by which the 1981 cuts were made by the UGC was vigorously attacked. Many academics felt it essential to ensure that 'future judgements, while certainly selective, would be carried out on the basis of criteria as far as possible known in advance to the university community' (Harris, M. 1986).

By 1986 the universities knew that the UGC was taking the research rankings (see Chapter 4) into account when making its decisions about resource allocations in a further period of constraint. However, the ways in which the research rankings were produced were not entirely clear and led to the plea for more explicit, objective PIs (for example, Sheppard, et al 1986; Rogers and Scratchard 1986; Evans and Clift 1987).

The pressure created by financial constraints not only leads to demands for a clearer identification of the criteria on which decisions on resource allocations are made but also encourages institutions to develop, or accept, PIs to show that they deserve a bigger allocation. Such pressures might be resisted by those institutions doing best under the current methods of allocation but the more likely result is an increase in the number of PIs advocated as the most suitable ones upon which to base resource allocations.

In its 1987 proposals that higher education institutions be required to seek funding on the basis of specific contracts the DES noted that measures of performance would be needed to ensure that institutions met their contracted output targets and suggested that more research would be required in this area.

Just as individual institutions have an incentive to gain a larger slice of the higher education cake, so the higher education system, at a time of financial constraint, has an added incentive to show that the system deserves a larger slice of the nation's resources than might be intended for it. According to the second statement from the CVCP/UGC Working

Group, 'several universities suggested that the development of performance indicators should be undertaken with an eye to strengthening the public image of the university system'. Page, a member of the Working Group's Technical Committee, thought that universities must adopt PIs because, 'if universities wish to receive increased sums of public money - and they must receive more - they must exhibit evidence that what has been received has been well applied' (*Times Higher Education Supplement*, 25 September 1987).

As was noted earlier, the proposals from the Jarratt Committee entailed a strengthening of the role of the management of institutions and PIs were advocated as one of the tools of management. Although evaluation has always been present in higher education, the introduction of PIs changes both how it is done, and who does it. Academics undoubtedly fear that evaluation may be taken out of their hands and used for purposes which they do not themselves determine. Moving the criteria from those of excellence determined by 'internalist' criteria intrinsic to the academic profession towards criteria related to discernible economic or other social outcomes inevitably moves the control of evaluation away from the academics towards the managers (Kogan 1989).

Nevertheless, in the present political climate the development of PIs has been accepted, albeit reluctantly. Anxiety now concentrates on choices of PIs and the use to which they might be put. Furthermore, some critics are concerned that as full a range as possible of PIs is used rather than a limited, possibly damaging, one. Some reports advocating use of PIs, for example, the Audit Commission report on public sector higher education (1986), claimed that the key PIs which were more generally accepted for higher education were cost per successful student; retention rates/success rates; staff-student ratios. But the adoption of such a narrow range of PIs would be a suspect procedure. In Chapter 3 we show how the cost approach can be valid if the assumption is made that the outputs of all higher education institutions are of equal quality, but this is a highly dubious assumption. The other way of validly using costs illustrates the need for a range of PIs because if costs are to be used as a PI then PIs for the quality of output of an institution should also be developed and introduced into the equation. The advantage of using a range of PIs is that different items are then taken into account and measured.

We have already seen that critics of the methods used in producing the UGC research rankings have argued for more objective PIs to be developed. With the UGC basing some funding decisions on its research rankings, pressure began to mount for the difficult task of assessing teaching quality to be tackled, to meet the danger that academics would devote more effort to research and less to teaching (Harris 1986).

Sizer foresaw some of these problems when, in 1979, he suggested that a wide range of PIs should be used because there might be a danger that 'in using short term output indicators of performance, such as cost per full-time equivalent student or cost per graduate, sight will be lost of the long term measure of the effectiveness of institutions, ie their contribution to the needs of society'.

The Development of PIs

The case for the development of PIs was then building up throughout the 1980s. Furthermore, as we shall see in relation to research PIs, one of the factors behind the development of such PIs was the technical developments in bibliometrics spearheaded by the Institute for Scientific Information at Philadelphia.

Considerable work was necessary before PIs could be adopted and in response to the recommendations of the Jarratt Committee, and the terms of the Concordat reached with the Government in return for the settlement of pay anomaly (See Chapter 1.1), the CVCP and UGC set up a Working Group on PIs. Its First Statement, *Performance Indicators in Universities* was published in July 1986 but it recognised that further work was required before the PIs could be fully implemented. It had been pressed to produce performance indicators during 1987 and could use only the information already available within the Universities Statistical Return (USR). Chapter 4 discusses the way in which the UGC started using some PIs to help with the implementation of the policy of selective funding of research.

The 1986 CVCP/UGC statement claimed to have sought to establish PIs which would assist universities in the internal management of their affairs and help the UGC and DES monitor university performance and the control of public expenditure. Teaching and research were said to be the major focus and the main aims were better accountability and the provision of management tools. The group found that all universities already had available information, much of which could be used effectively as PIs. The 16 most commonly used indicators were listed and over 70 others were used. Some of these, however, would not fall within the definitions of PIs discussed in Chapter 1. The statement recommended a range of PIs to cover inputs, processes and outputs and stressed that some PIs could play a particularly useful role in the identification of trends in performance.

The Working Group saw its principal task as being 'to standardise existing practice by formulating common definitions and developing an agreed list for use by all universities'. The need to introduce common PIs on a national basis as soon as possible caused them to look at some aspects of universities' work, in addition to teaching and research, where data were available for immediate implementation of valid and useful information. Each proposed PI was tested against a range of agreed questions including: was it relevant to the objectives of the organisation?; could it be quantified precisely and in an objective manner?; would it be of practical value to management of the organisation and to others outside the institution?; would it be acceptable?; were the data already collected satisfactorily?; what would be the cost in relation to benefit?

Where the relevant information was already available, some PIs were suggested for possible introduction in 1986/87. Another group was listed which could be implemented in the future and for which the information could be collected.

An interesting omission from the list was standards of entry to higher education (ie A level scores) with the statement acknowledging that 'it is known that the relationship between entrance score and degree class is weak'. This suggests a change of opinion from 1981 when A level entry scores were one of the main criteria used by the UGC. Harris, a member of the Working Group, took the argument a step further by suggesting that however difficult value-added is to measure, it, and not entry standards, is the relevant factor that should be used in judging university departments. The current renewed emphasis on widening access also make entry scores less justifiable as a performance indicator.

The statement advocated the development of teaching appraisal in all institutions and supported the use of student questionnaires but, apart from brief references to costs and wastage rates, did not specify which PIs they thought related to the teaching function. This might have seemed surprising given their implicit attempt to tackle Jarratt's comment about the lack of PIs for teaching by claiming to make it one of the main focuses of their work, and it was thought likely that the Working Group would return to the issue.

The Working Group claimed that 'this first statement has concentrated on creating an operational framework and on determining the mechanisms necessary for the implementation of performance indicators. There is still much work to do in devising specific indicators for a wider range of universities' work.'

Table 1. Initial Range of Performance Indicators Proposed in First Statement by CVCP/UGC Working Group

	Implementation Time Scale		
	1986/87	Near future	Future
Teaching and Research			
Cost per FTE student	X		
Research income	X		
Contribution to PG and professional training	X		
Submission rates for research degrees	X		
Number of research and sponsored students	X		
Occupation of graduates after 12 months	X		
Undergraduate wastage rates		X	
Occupation of graduates after 5 years			X
Analysis of publications/patents/agreements/copyrights			X
Citations			X
Peer review			X
Editorship of journals/officers of learned bodies			X
Membership of research councils			X
Costs per graduate			X
FTE students to FT academic staff	X		
Equipment costs per FT academic staff	X		
Others			
Administrative costs per FTE student	X		
Premises costs per FTE student	X		
Library costs per FTE student	X		
Careers services costs per FTE student	X		
Medical services costs per FTE student	X		
Sports facilities costs per FTE student	X		
Other central costs per FTE student	X		
Ratio of support staff to academics	X		

Future work envisaged by the group included attempting to distinguish the resource inputs to teaching and research. There is still a long way to go before all the PIs are fully developed and operational.

Later Cullen (a DES official) discussed a number of PIs that might help the government decide how far higher education was achieving its objectives but which had yet to be formulated in operational terms (Cullen 1987). He reiterated the 1985 Green Paper point that the government would be interested in the production of three main outcomes of higher education - highly qualified manpower, research and other social benefits - at maximum value for money but that as yet there was limited progress in developing PIs at a national level for the latter two. He concluded that, 'with the exception of recurrent cost per student, none of the indicators discussed in this paper yet has an established role in the monitoring and assessment of the higher education system'. As we saw in Chapter 1.2, the type of PI being discussed here is what the economists call cost effectiveness analysis and is used in many fields to work out the distribution of resources at a macro level.

In cases such as costs per graduate, the problem was more to do with the lack of information about public sector higher education than about the universities. Efforts were made to improve the collection of data; the Clayton Report (1987) proposed a new system for distinguishing teaching from research expenditure in institutions, though as noted above it is subject to major criticisms. Studies were also initiated to improve the estimates of non-completion rates.

There are also problems of application and technical problems because different institutions have differing aims. Cullen believed that one unresolved aspect of the use of PIs was the value added by the higher education process and the relationship between indicators such as the attainment of good degrees, subsequent employment success and the ability of students at entry to higher education. Cullen stressed that value added could play an important role in the comparison between the performance of different sectors of higher education and that the values added of the two sectors were not dissimilar. He concluded that despite the difficulties, 'perhaps the most striking development has been the growing and widening acceptance of it [performance measurement] at all levels in the higher education system'.

Inevitably interwoven with current discussions of PIs are the policy and funding initiatives pursued by the government. The 1985 Green Paper stated that 'an important thrust of research policy over the next few years will be towards selectivity and concentration'. The UGC research rankings were being used to implement this policy and yet in the humanities and social sciences there has been considerable disquiet about their rankings (Harris 1986). Many were looking to the development of more adequate research PIs to improve the reliability and validity of the UGC's research ranking exercise and, as happened in America, the production of reputational rankings is beginning to stimulate work on PIs that are claimed to be more objective. In its 1987 White Paper *Higher Education: Meeting the Challenge* the government welcomed the progress made by universities (including the CVCP's promotion of the development of PIs) to reassure the public about the ways in which they control standards. The contracts system, however, implies continued determination to monitor outcomes.

In the Second Statement (1987) the Technical Committee set up by the CVCP/UGC Working Group proposed that the 1984/5 and 1985/6 statistics which could constitute the data for 39 PIs should be published in the Autumn of 1987, as indeed they were. Of the 16 PIs that the First Statement had suggested could be implemented in 1986/7, seven were omitted: contribution to postgraduate and professional training; submission rates for research degrees; occupations of graduates after 12 months; medical services costs per FTE student; sports facilities; other central costs per FTE student; ratio of support staff to academics. Some of them cannot be implemented because there are currently inadequate means of collecting the information. This problem is not peculiar to the United Kingdom. Inadequate data bases constitute a very major problem in developing institutional assessment programmes in the USA.

In most cases, for example, library costs per student, several of the 39 PIs identified by the Technical Committee related to one of the 16 proposed in the First Statement for initial implementation. One of the seven 1986 PIs omitted from the list, ie occupation of graduates after 12 months, was re-designated as occupation of graduates after 6 months. The statistics were published under the title *Performance Indicators and Management Statistics*. This was a better title than *Performance Indicators* because, Page claimed, the term PIs, 'is an abbreviated way of referring to all those numerical data which are useful in managing a university, assessing its operations, costs and performance' (*Times Higher Education Supplement*, 25 September 1987). The Working Group noted that further work was required and that even the 1986 list was felt by some, 'to emphasise inputs and quantitative measures as opposed to outputs and qualitative results'. The Technical Committee also stressed, 'the need to be aware of the dangers of concentrating solely on the measurable and to neglect the wide range of qualitative factors which are impossible to quantify'. Nevertheless, the Working Group accepted that government pressure had created 'an imperative to produce a suite of indicators which could be published at the end of 1987'. This meant producing a list which overwhelmingly contained measurable input items and which was inevitably open to the question raised above about the validity of a list of PIs which does not give adequate attention to outcome measures. The list provided a good example of the point made by Carter (1989) that most PI systems in the UK are 'data driven' ie they are based on information already collected for other purposes. Similar criticisms have been made of the PIs used in the NHS (Allen, Harley and Makinson 1987).

Many of the PIs included also seemed open to the criticism that they failed to meet the point, hinted at in the statement, and noted in our discussion of the definition of a PI (Chapter 1), that the way in which the data are to be interpreted ought to be obvious. The Working Group's approach implied, although this was refuted, that lower costs were desirable but there was a danger of ignoring PIs concerned with the quality of the output. Thus, as we shall note in the next section, this approach is at odds with that sometimes adopted in the USA.

Despite these reservations and the pressure under which the work was completed, the Second Statement contained some sound analysis. The suggestion that PIs help to stimulate intelligent questions was important, as was the stress on trends rather than on a 'snapshot'. Such analysis was in line with general conceptualisations about the role of PIs within the public services as in, for example, Beeton 1988. Because of a redefinition of cost centres in 1984, a consistent data series was available only from 1984/85. The repeated warnings that PIs needed to be used carefully as an aid to judgement and not a replacement for it were also helpful and in particular the warning that 'uncritical use of these indicators may seriously damage the health of your university' has been frequently quoted. The Working Group praised the Technical Committee for so rapidly producing PIs for publication in 1987. They could, however, be criticised on the ground that emphasis may have been given to certain performance indicators simply because information is readily available. More significant PIs did not appear because of data collection difficulties. The result was a somewhat unbalanced list. It was noted that there was 'a radical change of direction in the aims of the working group between its first and second statements' (Elton, *Times Higher Education Supplement*, 11 September 1987). This claim was disputed by Page who went on to accept, however, that 'of course, there was an imperative to publish some useful figures by the end of 1987'. The prime reason, he made clear, was the need, already discussed, to illustrate that universities were properly spending the money they had already received and should therefore receive increased funding.

Current Perspectives

The list has become an annual publication and the management statistics and PIs appearing in the fourth volume, published in Autumn 1990, are given in Table 2. The list has been both extended and improved since 1987 but the items included in 1990 were identical to those of 1989. For example, as is explained in Chapter 3.5, the first destination indicators now take account of the differences between universities in terms of their subject balances. Undergraduate success rate indicators have been introduced - see Chapter 3.4 - as have indicators for entry qualifications.

Table 2. University Management Statistics and Performance Indicators, 1990

(Source: University Management Statistics and Performance Indicators, CVCP/UFC, 1990.)

Expenditure in Academic Departments
(by Cost Centre)

FTE Academic Staff
E1 Expenditure per FTE student
E2 Expenditure per FTE academic staff
E3 Expenditure on support staff per FTE academic staff
E4 Expenditure on equipment per FTE academic staff
E5 Research income per FTE academic staff

Students and Staff (by Cost Centre)

FTE Student Load
E6 Research postgraduates as a % of FTE students
E7 Taught postgraduates as a % of FTE students
E8 All postgraduates as a % of FTE students
E9a Ratio of FTE students to FTE teaching staff

Expenditure on central Administration

E10 Central administrative expenditure as a % of grand total expenditure
E11 Pay expenditure as a % of central administrative expenditure
E12 Central administrative expenditure per FTE student
E13 Central administrative expenditure per FTE academic staff

Expenditure on Libraries

E14 Library expenditure as a % of total general expenditure
E15 Publications expenditure as a % of library expenditure
E16 Library pay expenditure as a % of library expenditure
E17 Library expenditure per FTE student
E18 Library expenditure per FTE academic staff
E19 Expenditure on books per FTE student
E20 Expenditure on periodicals per FTE student

Expenditure on Computer Services

E21 Computer services expenditure as a % of total general expenditure
E22 Computer services pay expenditure as a % of total computer services expenditure
E23 Computer services expenditure per FTE student
E24 Computer services expenditure per FTE academic staff

Expenditure on Premises

E25 Total premises expenditure as a % of total general expenditure
E26 Premises pay expenditure as a % of premises expenditure
E27 Heat, water and electricity expenditure as a % of total general expenditure
E28 Cleaning and custodial services expenditure as a % of total general expenditure
E29 Repairs and maintenance as a % of total general expenditure
E30 Telephone expenditure as a % of total general expenditure

E31 Total premises expenditure per FTE student
E32 Premises pay expenditure per FTE student
E33 Heat, water and electricity expenditure per FTE student
E34 Cleaning and custodial services per FTE student
E35 Repairs and maintenance expenditure per FTE student
E36 Telephone expenditure per FTE student

Expenditure on Careers Services and Student Organisations

E37 Careers services expenditure per FTE student
E38 Grants to student organisations per FTE student

First Destinations of First Degree Graduates by Subject

E39 Destinations as at 31 December after graduation, UK totals by academic subject

First Destinations of First Degree Graduates by University

E40 Total graduates with known destinations
E41 Graduates with destination 'unemployed or short-term'
E42 Predicted value of indicator D41
E43 Difference between indicators D42 and D41
E44 Difference per hundred graduates

First Destinations: National Proportion of 'Unemployed or Short-Term' by Subject

Undergraduate Success (by Academic Subject Group)

E45 Number of successful leavers
E46 Successes as a % of those ending their studies
E47 Proportions on three and four year courses
E48 Terms of attendance per success
E49 E48 relative to expected value

Qualifications of Full-Time Undergraduate Entrants, 1987 to 1989 (by Academic Subject Group)

E50 Entrants with 3 or more A levels, numbers
E51 Entrants with 3 or more A Levels, scores
E52 Entrants with 5 or more Scottish Highers, numbers
E53 Entrants with 5 or more Scottish Highers, scores
E54 Entrants with other qualifications

The list is still open to many criticisms. In the Foreword of the 1989 Edition it is admitted that 'the title "University Management Statistics and Performance Indicators" continues to be used despite critical comments that "arrays of numbers do not become performance indicators just by being called so".' The inclusion of, for example, telephone expenditure as a percentage of total general expenditure is open to obvious criticism as in Johnston's (1989) review article, *Do You Use the Telephone Too Much? A Review of Performance Indicators, Evaluation and Appraisal in British Universities*. Moreover, as is admitted by Sizer (1989), a member of the Performance Indicators Steering Committee which produces the list, only two may be identified as being output or outcome measures and the set is more useful in assessing efficiency than effectiveness.

There was the usual general warning in the 1990 Foreword that users of the volume need 'knowledge, understanding and intelligence' and that 'careful interpretation' is vital if 'the data are to be the aid to good judgement which we intend'. The 1989 edition includes an illustrative commentary on the interpretation of some of the indicators along with the usual list of caveats.

Under the auspices of the steering committee, the technical work is undertaken by an editorial and development group and a Sub-Committee on Research Indicators (SCRI). A group is also developing a set of financial health indicators which they aim to publish in appropriate form in 1991. The work of SCRI is described in detail in Chapter 4. SCRI is part of the growing network of groups developing research PIs in the UK and it is considering the introduction of various research PIs into the CVCP/UFC list. Annual collection of data will begin in 1991 and some of them published soon after.

Following the Oxburgh Report in 1987 on Earth Sciences, similar reviews into a number of subjects were undertaken by the UGC. Although this procedure has now been abandoned, lessons can be learnt from the Oxburgh review in which departments were sent questionnaires which requested, among other items: a complete list of journal articles and conference papers; the number of publications per year; the number of citations received by these papers; and the number of highly cited papers per department.

1989 saw another research assessment/selectivity exercise conducted by the UGC/UFC which is also described in detail in Chapter 4. Although the procedure used was described as 'informed peer review', it was supported by a more systematic collection of research PIs than in 1986 and was subject to less criticism.

Ministers had been pressing the universities over a long period to give greater attention to teaching quality, and in 1988 the CVCP established a standing group under Professor Sutherland to create an academic standards unit to monitor universities' implementation of procedures for teaching quality assurance. Following a report from the Sutherland Group on academic audits, a unit has been established. It is proposed, however, that before visiting a university the 'audit team would *receive* an initial briefing based on performance and other quantitative indicators' (VC/89/160(a)) - (our emphasis). As Sizer argues, however, the unit 'cannot be expected to assess the comparative quality of teaching by subject areas in all universities. There is an important distinction between minimum quality assurance and comparative quality judgements'. Publishable PIs of institutional teaching quality are very difficult to develop (Sizer 1989, pp.10-15). Apparently the Joint CVCP/UGC PIs Steering Committee considered possible indicators but concluded that some used within institutions, such as classification of honours degrees, are inappropriate for making comparisons between institutions. It took the view that universities should undertake formal self-evaluation and appraisal of teaching as a matter of good practice, including the development of systems of individual teacher appraisal and student questionnaires. The committee intends to return to the issue of indicators of teaching quality.

Both of the new funding bodies, the PCFC and the UFC, have introduced new funding mechanisms in which the institutions are contracted to provide teaching following a bidding process. In Chapter 5 there is discussion of the potential role of PIs in helping the funding councils to make comparative judgements of teaching quality when awarding contracts, and when monitoring whether the quality contracted for has been delivered. Sizer (1989) claims that 'it has been suggested that the UFC should place on institutions, particularly those making low bids, unusual bids, and/or recruiting substantial numbers of fees only students, the responsibility to demonstrate fitness for purpose' (p.15). The use of published and internal PIs would be one element in demonstrating teaching quality.

PIs for UK higher education were mostly developed initially in the university sector. A report produced for the CDP in 1987/88 was not fully adopted. The public sector has recently, however, seen one of the most promising PI developments at the macro-level - the Performance Indicator Project (PIP) at Nottingham Polytechnic. A quarterly publication, *Print Out*, produced by Cliff Pettifor, provides information on questions such as: recent trends in cost, size and SSRs in polytechnics and colleges, and the extent to which cost is explained by variations in size and SSR; the extent to which student attainment indicators are explained by variations in expenditure (teaching and non-teaching), size and SSRs.

The political imperatives behind the development of PIs in the public sector were explicit. The Secretary of State sent a letter of guidance to the Chairman of the PCFC at the time of its incorporation in which he stated: 'I look to the Council to develop further indicators of both quality and quantity of institutions' teaching and would be grateful if it could consider how these might be used as an input to its funding policies and decisions' (Morris 1990, paragraph 1.2). The PCFC established a committee of enquiry, chaired by Alfred Morris, 'to suggest a range of indicators that might be used to assess the performance of institutions and advise how they might be used by the PCFC and the institutions themselves.' The Committee stated that it was in the interests of colleges and polytechnics to encourage the use of PIs because, 'this will help the PCFC to champion the interests of the sector, particularly in the context of its annual negotiations with the Secretary of State and the Treasury over the future scale of public expenditure on higher education in colleges and polytechnics' (paragraph 1.3).

It was stressed that information only becomes a PI when it is used to illuminate or measure progress relative to stated objectives. PIs are, therefore, 'the spotlights of a form of "management with objectives" in which a planning process provides the integrating framework for a system of institutional self-critical appraisal and review.' (paragraph 1.5). Having identified the limitations of PIs the Report reviewed the experience of the universities and the work on PIs by CNAA, NAB, CDP, Business and Technician Education Council (BTEC), and the Unit for the Development of Adult Continuing Education (UDACE), together with the recent reforms in the health service and the experience of the Scottish Education Department (SED). Although the PCFC Committee reviewed the findings of the CDP working party on PIs it was not jointly convened as the CVCP/UGC working party had been for the universities. On some topics, for example, in recognising that PIs are desirable but limited, the Morris Committee endorsed the work of the CVCP/UGC. However, its key findings about the use of PIs in universities were that, 'the CVCP performance indicators are of limited value to institutional managers; and that the best practice is found at institutional level when institutional comparisons are made using performance indicators which are integrated into the decision making processes of the university' (paragraph 2.5).

The Report noted (paragraph 2.21) that HMI are interested to note how and by whom PIs are collected, and what use is made of them. The judgements in their reports can be informed by the use of PIs. HMI have drawn several general conclusions about PIs from their inspections:

(a) institutions vary in the extent to which performance indicators are used;

(b) a lack of comprehensive and flexible information systems inhibits developments;

(c) indicators in use include: SSRs (common), unit costs (rare), non-teaching staff ratios (fairly rare) and space utilisation statistics (fairly rare);

(d) the most commonly used indicators are related to course monitoring and review procedures. There is little evidence of the systematic use or development of indicators relating to the quality of teaching and learning;

(e) institutions disagree about the usefulness of some indicators, for example: application rates and GCE A level point scores. To some extent, attitudes to specific indicators are determined by the kinds of students and courses offered by each institution;

(f) the cost and difficulty of collecting and using information is often seen as a barrier to their systematic and effective use;

(g) institutions find it more useful to compare their performance indicators with whose of other institutions facing problems of the same type rather than with those for the system as a whole.

Having outlined the key objectives of the Government and the PCFC, the Committee described the levels and purposes for which the PCFC needs PIs. At the sectoral or macro level they are needed to support the Public Expenditure Survey (PES) submission to the Secretary of State, and to illuminate progress towards the stated objectives of the Government and the PCFC. At institutional level indicators are needed by the PCFC to assist decisions on institutions' bids for recurrent funding and to form the basis of discussions with institutions on progress towards any particular objectives which may form part of the funding agreement between PCFC and an individual institution. The Committee is 'conscious that the Government is eager to stimulate competition between institutions and stimulate relevant aspects of a regulated market in higher education'. In stressing the importance of reconciling autonomy with accountability the Committee highlighted its belief that it should be for each institution to determine which PIs are most appropriate to its own internal management purposes, in the light of its distinctive mission and characteristics.

The outcome of the annual PES negotiations could be regarded as a collective 'public expenditure compact' between the sector and the Secretary of State. In the negotiations the PCFC, 'needs to be able to illustrate that the sector is well managed, accountable, performance conscious, a good investment and that its claims for resources are credible' (paragraph 3.34). Therefore the Committee recommended that the aims and objectives underlying the public expenditure compact should be made explicit and they might be illuminated by four sets of 'macro performance indicators' relevant to the stated aims and objectives of the government and the PCFC. These were:

(a) *Scale and effectiveness indicators*

Student population

Course completion

Student achievement

Value added

Employment and client satisfaction profiles

HMI and BTEC quality profiles

(b) *Level of resourcing indicators*

Index of revenue resource

Index of capital resource (equipment)

Index of capital resource (buildings)

(c) *Efficiency indicators*

Index of output cost

Ratio of students to staff

(d) *Source of funds indicators*

Ratio of public to total income

Ratio of private fees to public funds

Each PI was explained in detail. At institutional level, the Committee believed that to be effective, evaluation of performance must be rooted in its corporate planning process, through which the institution has set out its mission and objectives in terms which allow actual and planned performance to be compared. Institutions should share with PCFC, 'a confidential Executive Summary of the institution's corporate plan as the contextual basis for the PCFC's processes of monitoring, review and of competitive bidding for funds, contracting and performance monitoring' (paragraph 6.5). It was also suggested that the institutional funding agreement with PCFC might be reflected in an annual performance report.

The PCFC was recommended to introduce a rolling system of triennial institutional performance review visits. They would be the final stage in a process of institutional self-evaluation, the purposes of which would include, 'to review with the institution, its self critical appraisal of performance in relation to its mission statement and corporate plan and as illustrated by the institution's chosen performance indicators' (paragraph 6.10).

For a system of PIs to flourish the Committee believed a comprehensive range of statistics, ratios, costs and similar information is necessary. It therefore recommended, 'the establishment of an integrated Higher Education Statistical Record covering colleges, polytechnics and universities' (paragraph 6.15).

In many ways the PCFC Report followed the framework outlined in Chapter 1, with its stress on the importance of objectives and the use to which PIs should be put. In welcoming the Report the *Times Higher Education Supplement* (15 June 1990) said that one way to misuse PIs was to devise a set 'which fail to bite on day-to-day management . . . This sadly seems to be the outcome of the joint effort of the former University Grants Committee and the Committee of Vice-Chancellors and Principals to design appropriately discreet performance indicators for universities. The Treasury was suitably unimpressed.' It was suggested that the approach adopted by the Morris Committee should ensure a sensible context within which PIs would be used.

2.2 The United States of America

The contrast between the UK and the USA helps to explain the delay in the development of PIs in the UK. The American system is regarded as a 'mass' system with open access in contrast to the 'elite' system in the UK with its low age participation rate and high entry standards (Trow 1986; Fulton 1986). Although prestigious American institutions have high entry standards, the majority do not. Nor are the courses necessarily of the quality guaranteed by external examiners and common assumptions of standards in the UK. In America, therefore, some measurements that could be called PIs have been developed in order to judge standards and differentiate high ranking from lower ranking institutions. There was such diversity, even among the doctorate programmes that, according to Cartter (1966):

> 'Just as consumer knowledge and honest advertising are requisite if a competitive economy is to work satisfactorily, so an improved knowledge of opportunities and of quality is desirable if a diverse educational system is to work effectively.'

The basis of student funding and the pressure on public institutions from state legislatures might also contribute to this more consumerist approach in the USA.

The American 'non-system' of higher education 'is an extremely large, highly diverse patchwork of institutions that differ greatly in quality, in character, and purpose, in size and complexity, in fiscal stability, and in sources of funding' (Gardner 1985). In such a diverse system, with state agencies more influential than Federal in most cases, with undergraduate and graduate programmes often considered separately, and with a long and varied tradition of academic research into the quality of departments, describing the development and current use of PIs is a complex task. Most of the measures included in the original CVCP/UGC list of PIs for the UK have been collected in the USA, but although there are recent references to the term 'performance indicators' it does not seem to have been used consistently by Americans. The term was fairly popular in the early and mid 1970s but then for all practical purposes dropped out of the higher education literature (Miller 1987). Bourke noted that US policy use in this area 'is of relatively recent origin but it occurs in a context of extensive and long standing academic research in the field of quality/performance measures'. Probably more research is carried out at the technical level of developing equivalent measures in the USA than elsewhere. Thus Hüfner and Rau (1987, p.6) note that

> 'the US market type of interaction in higher education has led to extensive and long-standing academic research activities in the field of performance indicators . . . the experience gained in the US in developing, applying and modifying quality/performance indicators/measures in higher education . . . [serves] as a methodological-theoretical starting point for similar attempts in Europe.'

This remark illustrates the freedom with which outsiders can apply the term 'PI' to the US suggesting its absence in local discussion is merely a question of terminology rather than a result of the difference between the characteristics of American higher education and those of other systems. Such an interpretation is challenged by Kells (1989). He points out that although quantitative data are collected in the USA they are not akin to Western European PIs because they are used to inform peer review and to assist internal management and formative self-assessment rather than related to government goals and published in league tables that might influence funding decisions.

Hundreds of quality rankings of American institutions of higher education and their various departments have been published since the first in 1910. These rankings have employed dozens of methodologies, many of them only used once. Whilst a clear chronological picture does not always appear some general points emerge.

Although only a small proportion of the attempts to assess quality has been carried out as national reputational rankings, they have been the best known, have created a number of spin offs, and provide an interesting contrast with the UK. Unlike the UGC research rankings they have not been linked to specific policy initiatives. However, inevitably they have had an influence on funding and have improved the knowledge of students when making their choice of colleges. It was hoped that the information would be 'useful in strengthening graduate education across the country' (Cartter 1966).

The best known national reputational rankings include those of doctoral programmes published by the American Council on Education in 1966 (Cartter) and 1970 (Roose and Andersen) and the Carnegie classifications of 1976, 1979 and 1987 concerned with institutional rankings. Cartter provided a few objective correlates (eg publications, institutional backgrounds of faculty, faculty salaries, national graduate fellowships) for some of the departments and institutions but his was primarily a reputational ranking. Cartter found generally high correlations but, as is explained in Chapter 4.2, other researchers produced work suggesting 'no objective measure is linearly, or even monotonically, related to the Cartter ratings across fields' (Drew and Karpf 1981, quoting Beyer and Snipper 1974). The Cartter, and the Roose and Andersen studies generated a large amount of work on objective indicators of quality. Jordan (1989) suggests that the role of reputation in ratings is influential and the rating reports contribute further to the mystique of higher education, but not to its serious appraisal.

Objective Indicators of Quality

America has a much more extensive tradition in this field than has the UK and therefore much of the information for some of the later Chapters of this report comes from the vast array of articles in the USA reporting developments in the production of objective indicators. Much of the work concentrated on developing refinements to, or new versions of, bibliometric measures of research, ie publications and citations. Other objective indicators developed include: faculty awards, honours and prizes; scores at entry of students on standardised tests, eg Scholastic Aptitude Test (SAT) and the American College Test (ACT); students' achievements in later life; the academic background of the faculty; faculty salaries (eg Adams and Krislov 1978); institutional resources, eg expenditure per student, library holdings, physical plant, endowments, student-faculty ratios, research income earned.

The advantages and disadvantages of each of these, and the best way of measuring them, have been discussed at length elsewhere but several general comments might be made. In various combinations they have been discussed as part of the academic research tradition - the use of these indicators for policy making is discussed later. When the lists are discussed in general by some American authors such as Webster (1981) and Astin (1982) the natural inference is that the more generous the resources, the better the institution is doing. As we saw in Chapter 2.1, UK policy makers seem to take a different view, for at least some of the items such as staff-student ratios.

The significant development in the USA in the 1980s has been the growing preoccupation with one area of objective indicators, namely the quality of outcomes of undergraduate education. There has been a shift in professional research from ranking inputs to the study of effects. It has become increasingly clear that the measures used in the different studies reflect different constituencies with different stakes in higher education. Whereas peer evaluation and publications and citations rankings have come to be seen as expressing the producer's interest, outcomes' research reflects the realisation of the range of expectations held by different clients of the system - students, parents, employers, tax payers, policy makers. There is a growing belief that it is important to attempt to discover the benefits conferred by inputs and processes thought to be of high quality. There is widespread agreement that there is a growing concern with the assessment of quality and outcomes (see for example, Adelman 1986; Ewell 1985; Jordan 1989; Kells 1986) and with inter-institutional evaluation (Brinkman 1987). Brinkman and Tester (1987, p.6) suggest that one area for inter-institutional comparison is analysis of input and output data including: 'output patterns such as degrees awarded by field and level, research expenditure per faculty, percent of students graduating or dropping out; relative efficiency measures (or surrogates thereof) such as expenditures per credit hour or per student; and relative effectiveness indicators such as measures of value added or quality rankings.'

Jordan also notes that empirically generated data on outcomes could permit comparisons of campuses which use similar measures. After discussing how such comparisons might be used in for example 'a legislative debate on getting value for the investment of public funds' he notes that 'in some respects the matter is predetermined by the locus of authority'. He then makes one of the rare explicit American references to PIs: 'the term "performance indicators" may be used to bring to bear on students' learning econometric idioms and cost/benefit ratios. Such an approach may be methodologically driven when several institutions must be evaluated and the metric is not so much individual learners as aggregates in the thousand' (p.44). Despite such comments Jordan agrees with Kells that 'from the campus point of view, the major tool of academic assessment is self-study of a unit'.

In 1986 the Council on Post Secondary Accreditation issued new guidelines which required an assessment of outputs by institutions of higher education. Rogers and Gentemann (1989) show that in fact the accrediting agencies had already begun to add criteria that examined institutional effectiveness as measured by outputs. However, a survey they conducted in 1987 suggested 'an alarming lack of preparedness to demonstrate institutional effectiveness amongst colleges and universities.' Only 44 per cent of their sample had defined expected outcomes, and only a third had recommended or selected ways of evaluating the achievement of educational outcomes.

Major authorities in the field now maintain that even more than might have been the case previously a multidimensional approach should be used, whether for objective indicators, reputational rankings or a combination. Webster (1981) argued that 'there is room for debate about exactly what criteria should be used and whether and how they should be weighted, but at the very least, multiple criteria should be used'.

Solmon and Astin's major reputational study of undergraduate education (1981) asked respondents primarily in private colleges to rate each listed undergraduate department on six criteria:

(1) overall quality of undergraduate education;

(2) preparation of students for graduate or professional school;

(3) preparation of students for employment after college;

(4) faculty commitment to undergraduate teaching;

(5) scholarly or professional accomplishments of faculty;

(6) innovativeness of curriculum and pedagogy.

They then collected a range of objective data (eg student/faculty ratios, total enrollment size, percentage of graduate students, per student expenditure for various purposes) and correlated them with reputational rankings obtained using the six criteria.

The major recent multidisciplinary ranking of the quality of doctoral programmes was carried out through a multidimensional approach. In addition to the usual reputational rankings it included rankings of the programme's size, characteristics of its recent graduates, the size of its library and, in all fields bar the humanities, the research support and the recent journal articles produced by the faculty (Jones et al 1982). According to Fairweather (1988) this 'reputational rating of faculty quality has found widespread acceptance as a proxy for doctoral program quality' (p.346).

The multidimensional approach might come nearest to what the CVCP/UGC hope to achieve. One criticism of this approach is that even it does not relate the inputs to the outputs with sufficient precision. It is suggested that to do so a value-added approach is necessary.

The details of this approach, which compares the standards of the students leaving higher education with their standards on entry, are discussed in Chapter 3.2 but Astin, one of its long term advocates, claimed in 1982 that his 20 years' experience as a researcher conducting value-added studies had convinced him that

> 'funding agencies have never had much interest in supporting value-added studies and what little support there is seems to be waning. The argument here is not that these national studies have not proved useful or that they should not continue ... However, such studies frequently take a long time to produce useful results, and the results are often so general that they are difficult for individual institutions to apply to their particular problems'.

This situation has now changed, and throughout the 1980s a number of states (for example, Tennessee) have been or are attempting to make use of value-added (McClain et al 1986; Bogue 1982). It is increasingly recognised that 'approached in a comprehensive fashion, the issue of value-added to human lives by college can become the basis for claiming support from the polity' (Jordan).

Policy use

As we have already seen Bourke believed that PIs traditionally played a limited role in influencing policy makers in American higher education. This was despite the mission statements that provided institutions with objectives necessary for proper use of PIs and despite the amount of research on assessments of quality.

More recently, however, there has been greater use of PIs and this probably reflects such trends as the adjustments that American higher education had to make, after years of expansion and open access, to the fall in the number of students in the 1970s and the financial constraints. Faced with unlimited demand for service on one side and the harsh realities of public accountability on the other, the state colleges and regional universities are moving away from the rhetoric of education and towards the rhetoric of administration and management. Birnbaum (1985) claims that in these colleges, '"student credit hours per full time equivalent faculty" becomes a term heard as often in the faculty lounge as in the president's office; fiscal exigency, layoff, and retrenchment become parts of the argot as well as the environment, and discussion of access, quality and other core values is displaced by contingency planning, new management systems, and the need to collect data for external accountability purposes even though they may have little campus utility'.

Furthermore 'the quality control of higher education is also moving outside the academy' (Boyer 1985). Accreditation, which has always been a feature of American higher education is increasing, Boyer suggests. A typical list of items used in an accreditation process in the State of New York is cited by Gevers (1985). A comprehensive judgement, he suggests, is based on: the quality of the staff (PhDs, etc.); the amount of external grants; the number of publications and citations; the membership of professional associations; the quality of students (SAT scores, etc); the content of the curriculum; the employment of graduates; the library and computing facilities; the policy and support of top management for teaching and research; the interaction with other departments; and the centrality of the concern. In 1987 the US Secretary of Education restated the position that the award of Federal grants would depend upon successful accreditation, although this is already a foregone conclusion in 95% of cases.

In Ohio policies developed by the Board of Regents has enhanced the use of PIs. Funding had been based on uniform payment for standard service and designed to encourage access to higher education. The early 1980s saw financial constraints but a new policy in 1983 aimed at increasing the quality of higher education so that it would provide a resource for stimulating economic revitalisation. To find the centres of strength that were to receive the extra resources through competitive challenge grants the full range of PIs were used: reputational; inputs; outcomes; and value-added (Coulter and Moore 1987).

A value-added scheme is used in Northeast Missouri State University where quantitative measures are used to gain qualitative improvements (Taylor, T. 1985). A view is also developing in America that whether or not the institution practices evaluation is itself a useful PI. This approach is being actively considered in a number of state co-ordinating bodies which are responsible for advising legislatures on the allocation of funds to publicly supported state colleges and universities. Tennessee has the most developed version of this. The public authority does not make evaluative judgements but up to 5% of the annual allocation is now awarded on an institution's ability to demonstrate performances in five areas to which different weights are attached:

(1) the proportion of programmes which have received accreditations;

(2) the proportion of programmes which have undergone peer review or administered a comprehensive final examination to students taking a major over a five year period;

(3) value-added testing in the area of general education scores at the point of graduation;

(4) demonstration that specific changes have flowed out of earlier reviews;

(5) implementation of campus-wide plan for instructional improvement (Bourke 1986).

Student assessment of teaching in higher education has been a feature of American higher education but approaches such as this do not easily lend themselves to comparative judgements between institutions. However, Astin argues that institutions could be tested and scored in a manner similar to the approach used in Tennessee on a series of developmental questions such as:

(1) do students regularly evaluate their teachers? Are professors given student feedback in a non-threatening context that will maximise learning;

(2) do faculty members receive critical evaluations of their teaching from their peers;

(3) do academic advisers regularly receive student feedback?

These issues will be re-examined in Chapter 3 but illustrate once again that there might be valuable lessons to be learnt from America by the people with the responsibility for developing PIs in the UK.

2.3 Other Countries

Introduction

In the UK themes such as value for money, accountability, and strengthening institutional management have been seen to be important. Such concerns exist about other public services in the UK and in other countries. These concerns have led to the emergence of the 'Evaluative State' (Neave 1988). The rise of the Evaluative State involves a consolidation of previous evaluative activities and a shift towards *a posteriori* evaluation, which seeks to elicit how far goals have been met not by setting the prior conditions, but by discovering the extent to which overall targets have been reached through the evaluation of the product: '*A posteriori* evaluation works then through control of product, not through control of process' (p.10). This development involves, amongst other things, the 'multiplication of indicators of performance' and 'the judicious application of the econometricians' art'. The move towards expenditure-driven as opposed to demand-related budgeting has promoted performance related funding and encouraged PIs or quality assessments which permit finer targeting of resources (Neave 1987). The way that this has been applied in Holland is described by Maassen and Van Vught: 'The proposed use of PIs is an example of the way government wants to replace the former *ex ante* control mechanism of the performance of higher education institutions by an *ex post* evaluation mechanism' (1988, p.73).

Despite the existence of these general themes, systems of higher education vary in many ways including the degree of autonomy for institutions and individual academics. Furthermore within any one country different policies might be pursued for different sectors of higher education (as in the UK) or for different activities. Thus in Finland PIs are being used to allow greater autonomy to the undergraduate level of Finnish higher education, but to bring greater central co-ordination to the postgraduate level and research activities (Hölttä 1988).

It is also possible to identify life cycles of interest in PIs within different countries and public services (Pollitt 1989).

These factors mean that the development of PIs within countries varies greatly, as is confirmed in a recent OECD study (Kells 1990). The discussion occurs at two main levels; a policy making level and a technical level. Laying the groundwork in the former is critical. Thus Frackmann, having explained the failure of recent attempts in the Federal Republic of Germany (FRG) to introduce competition and selectivity by using PIs, concludes that before PIs are composed and structured, the conditions that are prerequisite for their use should be established: this is likely to involve political decisions. Similarly Kells (1983) suggests that quality control is a two stage process involving first, measuring quality and second, steering on the basis of the measurement recorded. Thus three main elements or variables emerge which can be examined and were used by Cave and Hanney (1989) when analysing the development of PIs in different countries: technical development; the political decisions to create structures to permit and encourage the use of PIs; and the adoption of policies which it is hoped PIs will be able to advance. Countries differ markedly in respect of the three variables.

The countries selected for discussion below illustrate many of the above points. The drive towards the Evaluative State is most advanced in Finland, the Netherlands, Sweden and the UK (Neave 1988). Hüfner (1987) believes the debate in the FRG on issues of differentiation, efficiency and effectiveness, accountability and PIs is at an early stage compared with the measures taken in Finland, France, the Netherlands or the UK. The two European countries identified by Teichler (1988) where performance or outcome measures have had most impact on policy and research are the UK and the Netherlands. Segers et al (1990) suggest that 'three countries took a leading position in the development of sets of performance indicators and pragmatic management technologies based on performance indicators: the United Kingdom, the Netherlands and Australia' (p.2). They go on to suggest that in all of these three countries there were two important Government papers, released almost at the same time and with a content that is surprisingly similar: the English and Australian Green and White Papers and the Dutch HOAK and HERP reports. It seems, they believe, 'there has been an extensive communication on these matters between government managers' (p.2).

The Netherlands

The Netherlands has seen possibly the most comprehensive debate about plans for the introduction of PIs, but implementation has proved difficult. The Chairman and Secretary of the Dutch Technical Working Party on PIs reported recently that 'the actual results of all the thought and discussion devoted to this subject in recent years is not, in fact, impressive. There has been a great deal of talk but very little has been achieved' (Mertens and Bormans 1990, p.95). It is also suggested that the use and life cycle of PIs are limited because 'the practice under consideration will change as a consequence of intelligent behavioural reactions of the organisation and people involved' (In't Veld et al, p.11). They also believe that more progress has been made in developing and applying indicators for academic research than for education in general.

Changes in the funding of research around 1980 at Leiden University forced departments 'to develop research performance criteria and, subsequently to apply these criteria in a sort of self-evaluation, in order to avoid a considerable decrease in research support' (Moed et al 1985, p.186). Subsequently the national system for university research financing changed from a 'dual support' type system to a 'conditional funding' system which was very similar to the Leiden scheme. According to Moed both the Leiden system and the national policy 'expressed a need for more objective, quantitative research performance indicators' (p.186). As a result a research project into bibliometric indicators started at Leiden in 1981. Some of its work is described later in Chapter 4.3.

The project showed that indicators could be used in several ways by different levels of university management. They could be fitted into the conditional funding system which involves research programmes being funded on condition their quality is guaranteed by the institution and favourably assessed by independent, external committees.

It is also argued that the government's role in the process of monitoring standards is above all a complementary one and as a result the performance of establishments must be made visible. It is thought that performance indicators can play an important role here if they are meaningful and acceptable to both parties. There is still much scepticism about this.

Developments in research form only a part of wider changes in Dutch higher education forced largely by economic pressures. In 1985 a government paper entitled *Higher Education: Autonomy and Quality* (HOAK) proposed self-regulation and autonomy as the new mechanism for steering higher education, and the development of a formal quality control system was regarded as an important condition for the transition from central control to self-regulation (Maassen 1987). In this move from *ex ante* control to *ex post* evaluation the representative bodies of the institutions played a role. The Association of Co-operating Universities in the Netherlands set up a Steering Committee which examined the development of various PIs and proposed their adoption. There was, however, opposition and the Association did not go ahead in the manner of its UK equivalent and introduce PIs. Considerable work was still necessary on the technical side before HOAK could operate and the PIs Research Group of the University of Limburg was appointed by the Minister to define quality, establish the conditions for quality assurance and to establish which indicators and variables are valid operationally (Dochy et al 1990). The research included sending a questionnaire to a range of stakeholders asking for opinions about which out of a number of indicators and variables identified were considered to be valid measures. The findings are intended to be used as the starting point for an attempt to develop a shared language.

The new quality control system being developed in Holland involves a number of stages: self evaluation by the faculties; comparison between faculties made by visiting review committees, and a response by the institution to the committee's findings. The development and use of PIs within this quality control system has been controversial and difficult. Several commentators (see, for example, Bormans et al 1987) stress the importance of PIs in the dialogue between the Higher Education Institutions (HEIs) and the government. The HOAK scheme is being implemented in the *Higher Education and Research Plan* (HERP). Dialogue is important in HERP and In't Veld et al argue that PIs 'can stimulate a dialogue that is precise and fruitful because PIs can back statements with the relevant facts . . . we also expect that PIs will not only make the dialogue more to the point, but will also provide an incentive to make the qualitative reasoning more precise, because the qualitative reasoning has to compete with supposedly objective facts, which seem to be *a priori* convincing' (p.13/14). This role for PIs is further discussed in Chapter 5.

The government, according to Maassen and Van Vught (1988) attempted to establish a major role for PIs in HERP. It set out structures for the deployment of PIs and proposed a number of policy uses for them within the system of internal and external evaluation being established. According to the Government PIs would serve as operational instruments for: evaluation (to show to what extent Government goals had been achieved); monitoring (to signal relevant developments and trends); dialogue (to provide an objective basis of information); and funding. Maassen and Van Vught question the extent to which the new system will enhance the autonomy of institutions and suggest that 'the ways these indicators are intended to be used make it very clear that this new system of quality control is as invasive for the institutions as was the [former] system' (p.73).

Kells (1989) stresses that it is the Government which has been pushing for the introduction of PIs and doing so in relation to government goals for higher education, but that concentration on this by some British commentators has underestimated the main thrust of policy which has been the establishment of the systematic, cyclical, developmental, self-assessment and regular site visits by subject matter peers and lay citizens.

In 1988 a tentative matrix of 26 indicators was published in HERP. For each of the 26 a ranking order between the universities was given. There were many criticisms of the indicators, especially the fact that for those where a time series was given account was taken of only the changes per institution in their relative position compared to others. This reflected badly on the universities which were performing well initially. There were also doubts about what some of the PIs were intended to measure.

Australia

Although four Australian institutions took part in the OECD survey, Bourke referred to 'the virtual absence, in the very considerable literature of higher education research in Australia, of any sustained work on performance indicators, quality measures and the like' (para 2.6). However, following a Government Green Paper the bodies representing leaders of higher education institutions - the Australian Vice-Chancellors' Committee (AVCC) and the Australian Committee of Directors and Principals (ACDP) - set up a Joint Working Party on PIs 'to develop a set of PIs which would be acceptable to the Government' (AVCC/ACDP 1988). In its White Paper of the same year the Government stated that 'as soon as practicable, indicators which are agreed to be useful and appropriate will be incorporated into the Commonwealth's general funding arrangements for higher education' (quoted in AVCC/ACDP 1988). The Joint Working Party thus had the incentive to conduct the technical work to develop a list of PIs that could be tested and then used. Their report opposed the use of PIs by the Government 'in any purely mechanical fashion as in formula funding' but recognised that they have a place in financial matters and that given the need for institutions to be made accountable and transparent by a process of expert review 'performance indicators form part of the necessary raw material of evaluation and assessment'.

The Working Party set limits on what should be regarded as a PI. Although it listed some indicators of institutional context it reserved the term PI (in respect of teaching and research) for: students' evaluations of teaching and curriculum; completion rates; destination and acceptance of graduates; and research grants and publications.

A Higher Education Performance Indicators Research Group was established to define in operational terms, and conduct an empirical trial of, the indicators identified in the Working Party report. Those considered feasible and appropriate would be applied system-wide (Linke 1990). A description of the progress made on student evaluations of teaching is given in Chapter 3.7.

Federal Republic of Germany (FRG)

The first pilot study of PIs in West Germany was in 1975/76 and the idea for the OECD survey noted above followed proposals from a German research team. In 1983 the Federal Minister for Education and Science introduced a new policy in a document entitled, *Competition Rather than Bureaucracy*. It demanded less state intervention and more market mechanisms and stated: 'the higher education institutions have to acquire an interest in the specific performance they offer in the competition' (quoted in Hüfner 1987a, p.136). The influential Science Council published detailed suggestions in 1985 for introducing competition. Internal judgements of individual institutions based on a list of proposed PIs were to be followed by an evaluation by the scientific community, the results of which would be the determining factor in the resource allocation process (Hüfner and Rau 1987). Partly as a consequence of these debates many surveys were published on differences of quality and reputation between universities or within disciplines (Teichler 1988).

Evidence from Hüfner (1987) and Frackmann shows that when the OECD survey was conducted in the mid-1980s only limited use was being made of PIs beyond those 'operating' PIs required by the Lander for state planning mechanisms. Further, some of the measures that might have been in use were not recognised as PIs.

Therefore despite some developments in techniques and ideas for policy use in the FRG, Frackmann is probably correct in arguing that the attempt to introduce competition and selectivity by using PIs have failed because the structures for the use of PIs have not been adopted or imposed. In contrast to the UK and Australia, the organisation representing the heads of institutions did not feel under sufficient political pressure to introduce a recommended list of PIs. Hüfner (1987a) concludes that 'the willingness of universities to develop systems of performance indicators which go beyond those prescribed by the state is almost zero because further financial cuts and/or a further narrowing of institutional autonomy might occur . . . The actual application of different sets of PIs between and within institutions of higher education remains primarily a political decision' (pp.140-1).

Finland

Recent experience in higher education in Finland is both of expansion, involving an increase in resources in 1987 of 13% to 14%, and of a drive for improved efficiency reflecting international trends in higher education management. There is an awareness of the importance of information in management and planning as well as awareness of cost. Jäppinen (1987), a Ministry of Education official, maintains that 'a need has arisen to connect evaluation of performance with resource planning more rationally'. The Finnish Ministry of Education has sought to make higher education socially more relevant and economically more efficient, both by increasing direct public accountability through a formal evaluation system and by encouraging institutional leadership and academic self-regulation (Hölttä 1988).

In 1984 the Ministry for Education set up a working group to survey existing methods of evaluation and to propose methods of evaluating the output of the education process both in qualitative and quantitative terms. The working group submitted its report in 1985 concluding that 'evaluation of performance of higher education is necessary'. The central focus of evaluation is to assist internal decision making. Furthermore, 'in order to give the universities more responsibility over the financial matters they should be given the possibility to allocate personal and other resources in an essentially freer way'. The main targets of evaluation are taken to be each individual university and research, field by field, at a national level.

On the evaluation of teaching the working group concluded that only quantitative efficiency and not qualitative efficiency could be measured on the basis of present information. Quality may be improved by period on period revision of curricula based upon peer opinion. In terms of input/output ratios it was argued that 'it is not necessary to develop many different indicators, but only a few that can be commonly applied as such in every university and in every faculty' (Jäppinen 1987). The working party called for care in the definition of concepts and in the interpretation of results.

Structures were developed to allow greater evaluation. The Development Act of 1986, which came into force in 1987, stated that all HEIs would apply a system of performance evaluation producing sufficient and comparable data on output and costs of institutional activities. In 1987 a data base was published. The Act was intended to improve conditions for goal-orientated management and increase 'the possibilities of higher education institutions independently to decide on the use of funds allocated to them' (Ministry of Education 1986). Research was to 'be made systematic and planned'. In practice, however, there are difficulties and limitations at the technical level and 'indicators that yield information about research activities have been particularly hard to find' (Hölttä, p.99).

Although the system of evaluation is still evolving, the principle of rewarding efficient institutions and departmental behaviour is already being applied. Institutions receive the additional funding partly as an incentive, on the basis of their performance in the production of graduates, but particularly in regard to research and postgraduate research training. The Finnish Government will require reports on performance. Initially, very few PIs were to be used - for research performance the only indicator originally included in the database was the number of doctorates awarded (Taylor, M. 1989). However, a comprehensive range of research PIs is being added to the database (Niiniluoto 1990).

Sweden

In Sweden, although some work is being undertaken at the national level, there is no system-wide adoption of PIs: some faculties, however, within institutions are experimenting with them.

There has, however, been considerable work on self-evaluation (Furumark 1981, Sizer 1982). The National Board of Universities and Colleges inaugurated a project on institutional self-evaluation to reinforce the 1977 reform which was intended to lead to a more decentralised system. It was thought that, since these changes would take place without increased resources, in order to preserve their autonomy institutions will have to improve their capacity for self-renewal and reappraisal of existing programmes. A centrally sponsored project was thus initiated to foster self-study and self-evaluation. This was part of a swing away from the centre-periphery, social engineering reform strategy towards a more dynamic, process-oriented perspective, where self-evaluation and the capacity for self-renewal are key concepts (Furumark 1981).

It was thus not intended that the process should be for the benefit of central decision making but for the departments and institutions themselves. The project was therefore inaugurated through a series of events encouraging institutions to participate. These included workshops in which, for example, simulation exercises in trimming budgets highlighted the difficulties of coping with goal conflicts and finding criteria and measures of quality and relating them to economic realities.

In some universities self-evaluation has become part of the annual budgetary process and others refer to the process in stating their plans.

Swedish policy has not yet gone firm on the kind of performance information that will be sought. A government Bill in 1988 said that all levels of the system 'must develop reasonable yardsticks . . . showing how Swedish higher education and research are placed by international comparisons.' But they appear to fall short of procedures that will rank institutions and continue to be concerned that quality control will be linked to the active processes of higher education (Bauer 1990).

2.4 Some Comparative Points

The uses of PIs in the seven countries described in this Chapter are at different stages and despite some common general themes, occur within the settings of different political and educational objectives. There is, however, no clear correspondence between characteristics of systems and the use of performance indicators. Indeed, when some of the developments are compared, paradoxes emerge which lead to the conclusion that the introduction of performance indicators may be adventitious, or may be used in different places to advance quite different ends.

Thus, in the United Kingdom, PIs are seen as a way in which a hitherto liberally administered system can now enforce higher standards of academic performance and more economic use of resources. They are clearly tied to notions of public accountability and form part of a major reconstruction of relationships and modes of decision making between the state, the central funding agencies created by the state, and the management of individual HEIs.

By contrast, in Finland, the legislation incorporates PIs as part of a revised structure for financing universities but, starting from a system in which central control has been detailed and prescriptive, the authorities claim that PIs will enhance rather than reduce the freedom of universities. This claim is echoed in proposals made for the FRG and for the Netherlands. The argument seems to be that to apply objective indicators will both free universities from the more traditional, detailed and subjective processes of making a case for funds and establish clear rules of the game and a structure of incentives within which HEIs can operate. PIs thus create a system of given rewards akin to the prices given in the market. Hüfner (1987) argues similarly that, 'in theoretical terms, it can be said that the more decentralised/less government-controlled and the more competition/market orientated a national university system is, the larger the necessary number of performance indicators will be'. Neave (1988) shows that the impact of the general background themes described earlier varies: 'in systems based on decentralisation, the Evaluative state appears as a step towards greater central control and, in those based on a higher degree of centralisation, it is perceived as giving rise to greater flexibility and hence decentralisation' (p.11).

Analogies with the operations of the free market also apply at another level. Bourke (1986) usefully makes comparisons between the USA and the UK. In the USA, there is prolific provision offered by a wide range of institutions in which state control of public institutions goes alongside a strong regard for the power and rights of the consumer to have information about the institutions for which he is either paying fees or taxes or both. Thus Bourke maintains that in the USA the primary impulse towards using quality indicators has been a market pressure to provide consumer information, although there has been pressure from the desire to be economic from international competitiveness. The mixed private and public market there constitutes in his terms 'a very substantial free market of institutional preferences and choice'. Within such a market information is valued.

A further strand is the use of PIs for purposes of professional development. Bourke advocated this in Australia and this theme was taken up by the AVCC/ACDP Report. It is also important in Sweden. PIs have also been linked in a number of countries with moves towards increased selectivity in research. Taylor, M. (1989a), shows that in many countries the balance has shifted from 'indirect' funding of research, where an institution employs its general funds or block grant for research in areas chosen by its own staff, to 'direct' funding where particular projects are funded on the decision of external bodies, with a greater or lesser degree of immediate governmental influence or control. In countries including the UK, the Netherlands and Australia there is a debate about the role PIs can, and should, play in the implementation of such a process.

It will thus be seen that performance indicators, as other managerial devices, are tied up with systems rather than individualistic thinking, but are not necessarily shaped by a particular style of policy concern. The enhancement of managerial control, the opening up of institutions to consumer review, and the strengthening of professional judgements assisting the introduction of research selectivity, are all motives that have been advanced.

The picture is further complicated by the fact that a policy such as increasing the role for institutional management may, as with the general rise of the Evaluative State, take place in systems where the central government had previously had considerable influence over higher education and/or in systems where there had traditionally been considerable autonomy for the individual academic. Therefore, similar policies may be viewed very differently in different systems.

Furthermore, policies might not achieve what the government suggests they are intended to achieve or they might be open to various interpretations. As we have seen Maassen and Van Vught suggested that this was happening in Holland in an article entitled *An Intriguing Janus-Head: The Two Faces of the New Governmental Strategy for Higher Education in The Netherlands*. Van Vught's (1988) wider analysis covered other countries and suggested that moves towards greater autonomy for institutions were somewhat spurious; instead, with the development of PIs, governments were attempting to use new methods to steer the higher education system towards its desired goals.

The situation in the UK is also the subject of a debate in which some see the development of PIs as part of a move towards centralisation and others (for example Sizer 1989) see it as giving greater autonomy to institutions. This point is further discussed in Chapter 5.

One common theme in the development of PIs is that their introduction is controversial. There have been various attempts at an 'official' national level or at the level of an individual institution to test the validity and/or acceptability of different PIs by assessing the attitude of lecturers etc. towards them. In addition to the Limburg project in Holland other smaller exercises have been described by Moses (1985) in Australia and Rutherford (1987 and 1988) at Birmingham University.

Chapter 3

Surveys of Performance Indicators of Teaching

3.1 Assessing Teaching Performance

The ideal performance indicator for teaching would establish a relationship between all the benefits of the educational process, and all the relevant costs. Outputs include increases in the earnings potential of graduates associated with possession of a degree, other benefits to graduates which are not reflected in earnings potential, and the worth of the educational experience itself. Each of these outputs should be measured as the difference between an individual's experience as a graduate and the experience of an identical non-graduate. The outputs should then be related to inputs specific to the institution's teaching functions.

We discussed in Chapter 1.3 one method of attempting this procedure, that is, by computing the private or social rate of return to investment in higher education. As noted there, the technique captures only some of the benefits, and it adopts special assumptions about the allocation of costs between teaching and research. It is also applicable only at a high level of aggregation, and is thus incapable of discriminating between different institutions. This chapter discusses other more restricted but also more practical means of assessing teaching performance through performance indicators.

In the 1970s Birch, Calvert and Sizer (1977) explored the potential for developing PIs for teaching. They claimed that even if the inevitable generality and vagueness of the objectives of higher education were accepted, it was possible to move directly to the measurement of output, or perhaps more exactly, the outcomes of higher education: 'enrolments, pass and attrition rates and information on graduate employment by course are all indicators of society's response to the institution's provision of learning opportunities, ie they are outcome measures.' Although value-added was seen as a more sophisticated measure of output, it was not possible to use it in the project. As a measure of the input-output relationship, ie of efficiency, they suggested that one possible approximation of unit cost was the student-staff ratio and that a number of variables needed to be considered when working this out. Despite their work, as recently as 1985, the UGC, in a Circular Letter, told universities:

> 'Research can be assessed through peer judgement and a variety of performance indicators, but there are few indicators of teaching performance that would enable a systematic external assessment of teaching quality to be made.' (UGC, 22/85.)

This was a restatement of the traditional view, expressed in the Leverhulme Report (1983), that 'it is difficult to determine how well an academic is carrying out his teaching activities except in cases of serious dereliction of responsibility'.

Acceptance of this argument created the risk that teaching quality would decline as institutions became aware that it had no impact on allocations. There is evidence from a number of countries of both increasing pressure to appraise teaching, and yet, in practice, increased emphasis being given to performance in research. The previous chapter revealed that in a number of countries the funding for research is becoming increasingly selective rather than being linked automatically to student numbers. This creates the danger that unless teaching is also assessed all available effort will be diverted to 'grant earning' research activities and teaching will receive less attention. In these circumstances Elton (1987) claimed, 'The UGC decision not to use teaching quality in its resource allocation is inevitably going to lead to a decline in its quality'. A lecturer from Sheffield whose geology department was due to close as a result of the Oxburgh Report and the UGC's restructuring exercise thought that its lower than average research rating was the penalty for three 'misdemeanours' including allowing 'too much staff effort to go into undergraduate teaching with a wide range of course options' (Carswell 1988).

The Chairman of the Australian Research Council, Don Aitken, recently said that teaching in Australian universities needed to be restored to a place of honour and taken much more seriously by academics. Universities were essentially funded as teaching institutions, yet research was given much more status and priority. The reasons for this included: 'the best research advances knowledge; research is easier to evaluate than teaching; research is an international activity while teaching is local; excellence in research will get you promotions faster than excellence in teaching' (*Times Higher Education Supplement*, 9 March 1990).

Similarly in America Miller shows that performance in research has become increasingly more important than teaching performance when promotion and tenure decisions are being made.

Despite, or perhaps partly because, of these developments, there is increasing pressure to appraise teaching performance. A recent report in the *Times Higher Education Supplement* (Boyer, 9 February 1989) claimed that lecturers were pressing for this in the USA. There have been developments in Australia (Moses 1989) and in New Zealand where Clift et al (1989) described a scheme introduced in 1988 at Victoria University of Wellington whereby all academic staff applying for promotion have to submit evidence of their teaching competency.

In the public sector in the UK there already exists more of a teaching quality assessment culture than in the universities. There are various reasons suggested for this: the accreditation procedures of the CNAA; the role of the HMI; and the fact that 'research is not a primary concern for the majority of academic staff' (Sizer 1989). There was some dispute about the extent to which HMI reports could be used to inform PCFC funding decisions. However, as the PCFC (1990) Report, *Recurrent Funding and Equipment Allocations for 1990/91*, explained, the Programme Advisory Groups (PAGs) relied mainly on the HMI evidence when deciding whether to accept an institution's claim that it provided education of a high quality in the programme area and should thus be eligible for the quality discount on its bid price. Where the institutions agreed, evidence from BTEC, based on their moderators' assessments, was also made available to the PAGs. The Morris Report took the debate further and recommended that an HMI quality profile and a BTEC moderator profile should be developed as PIs. For the universities in the UK, the Jarratt Report commented that although the UGC had no present intention of taking quality of teaching into account, because it had no reliable way of assessing it, the situation 'may change when satisfactory PIs for teaching are developed'. Indeed, only a year later (1986) the UGC, in its joint working party with the CVCP, suggested that PIs should and could be developed for the two main functions of universities, teaching as well as research.

The 1987 White Paper (DES 1987) endorsed the view that the quality of teaching should be evaluated. It suggested that the maintenance of high standards of teaching could be helped by 'systematic arrangements for: staff training and development; staff appraisal; evaluation of the results achieved, including analysis of external examiners' reports and students' employment patterns; involvement of professional practitioners in vocational courses; and feedback from students themselves'.

The White Paper went on to suggest that the quality of teaching needed to be judged by reference mainly to students' achievements. Items that provided some measure of teaching quality included: non-completion rates; the subsequent employment patterns of students; and students' achievement compared with their entry standards. A similar list of PIs appeared in the Report from the NAB's Good Management Practice Group (1987).

The ministerial pressure referred to earlier included a speech in 1988 by the then Secretary of State for Education, Kenneth Baker, in which he stated 'effective teaching needs to be identified, highly prized, encouraged and rewarded' (Baker 1988). In the face of such pressure the Sutherland Standing Group was established partly as a defensive mechanism to help ensure HMI were not introduced for UK universities as they had been for those in the Netherlands (Sizer 1989). We have noted that the audit teams would receive 'an initial briefing based on performance

---

Table 3. Draft Outline Checklist for Academic Audits

The following areas of universities' quality control mechanisms could be monitored by the Academic Audit Unit.

1. Centrally planned monitoring of courses and teaching.
2. Scrutinising new courses or degree programmes (or revisions of them).
3. Monitoring existing courses and degree programmes, including data collection, such as student numbers, drop-out rates, classified degree results, etc.
4. Monitoring teaching (including lecturing, tutoring, practical supervision, etc).
5. Monitoring postgraduate training and research, including appeals procedures at postgraduate research degree level.
6. Assessing and monitoring the work of academic staff.
7. Staff development.
8. Seeking external examiners' views.
9. Dealing with external examiners' reports.
10. Seeking students' views on courses.
11. Monitoring and informing students of their progress.
12. Seeking views of external bodies - professional accrediting bodies, and employers, etc.
13. Validation by the university of courses in associated institutions.
14. Promotion of innovative practice in universities such as use of interactive video and expert systems.

Source: CVCP, VC/89/160(a), Annex A (Sutherland Report).

and other quantitative indicators and descriptive material' (VC/89/160a). However the draft checklist of the areas of universities' quality control mechanisms that could be monitored by the academic audit unit (see Table Three) contains comparatively few PIs. The list is drawn from the Reynolds Report and various CVCP codes of practice.

Not only do there appear to be comparatively few PIs in this list but the difficulties faced by the CVCP/UFC Steering Committee in developing publishable institutional PIs for teaching quality have been described above and Sizer (1989) concluded that 'to date, publicly available PIs of comparative teaching quality are little more than a desirable objective'. An equivalent attempt by the PCFC (Warnock 1990) appears to have made no more progress in detailing specific PIs although it did recommend six strategies designed to enable institutions to demonstrate the quality of their teaching.

Despite these difficulties it is possible to identify PIs that relate to the teaching function, even though in most cases it is indirectly so. The CVCP/UFC does not indicate which of its suite of PIs it believes are related to the teaching function and which to the research function. Clearly any rigid division between teaching and research is inappropriate but this chapter discusses a number of possible PIs that could relate to the teaching function. A major issue is the extent to which they could be considered to be valid indicators of teaching performance.

Miller (1986) lists the many sources of information used to evaluate teaching in American colleges. These range from systematic student ratings, examination performance and peer review to alumni opinions and long-term follow up. Some colleges have also pioneered procedures for estimating the value-added of particular institutions. However, as was noted, whilst the term 'performance indicator' was fairly popular in the early and mid-seventies, for all practical purposes it has dropped out of the higher education literature in recent years (Miller 1987). Despite this the present chapter draws on both British and American experience to survey the range of performance indicators of teaching.

3.2 Measuring Output: Value-added

When evaluating the outcome of teaching, the traditional approach has been to examine students and categorise their final level of attainment into various grades, for example, by looking at degree classifications. The higher the level achieved, the better the outcome of the education process. Taylor, T., (1985) notes that:

> 'Traditions have developed that . . . reward students through normative, highly competitive (with others, not oneself) grading practices that disregard individuals' starting point differentials and concentrate, instead, on output differentiations among people.'

The implication of the traditional approach is that, for the same costs, institutions which produce students of a higher achievement level are doing better. This approach to the evaluation of the teaching process has been increasingly criticised in recent years. Egan (1986) traced the development of an American reaction against lists showing the top HEIs by the achievements, for example, in later PhDs, of their graduates. Research has shown that the top fifth of HEIs had above average quality inputs and that therefore 'these top 50 HEIs make or earn or acquire their reputation because of what happens in the admissions office rather than by what happens in the classroom' (p.10). This type of reaction evolved into the value-added testing and measurement movement. In America, particularly, attention has been given to the measurement of the 'value-added' to an individual as a result of undergoing education. Astin (1982) writes:

> 'The basic argument underlying the value-added approach is that true quality resides in the institution's ability to affect its students favourably, to make a positive difference in their intellectual and personal development.'

In 1986 Egan claimed that 'value-added testing and measurement is a new but increasingly important movement in Higher Education' (p.1). It offered HEIs which were not amongst the top rated ones 'the opportunity to document the real educational opportunities that they instinctively know are taking place on their campus' (p.14).

Until recently the value-added approach has not been taken up in the UK. On the contrary, it is students' A-level entry scores that have been used as a performance indicator and higher scores have been associated with better performance of institutions and departments. Entry scores are a measure of student demand and show how different institutions fare in the market place as represented by potential entrants. But higher A-level scores reflect only higher academic levels on entry, and unless value-added is demonstrated in some other way they may provide no evidence on what the institution has added to the students' capabilities or performance.

There is a wide variety of evidence concerning the relationship between students' entry standard scores and final degree performance. In view of the debate about performance indicators the literature has been reviewed recently by Barnett (1988) and Johnes and Taylor (1987). Some of it suggests that there is a weak or non-existent relationship. This can be interpreted as meaning that A level entry scores are a poor measure of students' actual level of attainment in areas relevant to their studies, though other interpretations are possible too. Nonetheless, entry scores tend to take on a rather ambiguous quality when value-added is considered an appropriate indicator.

Using regression analysis to test a set of explanatory variables of variations in degree results between universities, Johnes and Taylor (1987) concluded that 'degree results are strongly influenced by both student-related and university-related factors, but none of these relates specifically (as far as we can tell) to the quality of teaching' (p.598). Somewhat at odds with previous research based upon detailed surveys of individual graduates they found that the mean A level score of a university's students is highly significantly related to degree results. They argued that it was possible to obtain a predicted degree result for each university which standardised for inter-university variations in the explanatory variables (which included as the most significant ones, A-level score of entrants; percentage of students living at home during term; Scottish universities; percentage graduating in arts subjects; percentage graduating in medical sciences; library expenditure as a total of expenditure). The difference between the actual and the predicted degree results would then indicate how far differences between universities had not been explained by the variables included in the model. They concluded that

> 'Clearly, some other variables are responsible for the remaining 'unexplained' variation in degree results and one of these variables may well be teaching quality. But it would be extremely rash and cavalier to assume that the unexplained variation in degree results could be attributed to teaching quality' (p.599).

Trends favouring the measurement of value-added can be detected recently in the UK, particularly at the instance of the PCFC and CNAA. In the 1987 White Paper (DES 1987), it was maintained that 'Academic standards and the quality of teaching in higher education need to be judged by reference mainly to students' achievements', and that 'Evaluation of institutional performance also requires students' achievements to be set alongside entry standards.' Whilst the White Paper asserts that what needs to be measured is not only improvements in specialist knowledge but also in communication skills, and in positive attitudes towards enterprise and employment patterns, there are indications in the White Paper and in the work carried out by NAB and CDP that the desire to measure 'value-added' may be translated into simply looking at the differences between A level scores and degree results. This is sometimes thought to be an inadequate measure of value-added - as we shall see below - and it also entails assumptions which are open to question (Bligh et al 1980; Barnett 1988). Nonetheless, in view of the current political interest in widening access to higher education, value-added measures are likely to receive greater attention even though they do not figure in the current CVCP/UGC list of indicators for annual collection. Furthermore at a general level the concept of providing added value to their students is attractive to most higher education lecturers. Thus Halsey's 1989 survey of higher education lecturers suggests 'that universities and polytechnics see themselves as capable of giving considerable added value to the ability of the students they admit from the secondary schools' (*Times Higher Education Supplement*, 16 February 1990). From a Dutch perspective also Dochy et al (1990) conclude that more research on PIs such as 'value-added' is desirable.

The increasing level of research in the UK on devising value-added schemes based on entry and exit qualifications is beginning to produce results. Such an approach was used to make a comparison between the value-added by British universities and polytechnics (Bourner and Hamed 1987). The most significant work is the jointly funded PCFC/CNAA project commissioned by the Morris Committee to, 'test different approaches to the measurement of value added, and . . . determine a methodology for the calculation of value added, based on a comparison of entry and exit qualifications' (PCFC/CNAA 1990, paragraph 1.2). This was acknowledged to be 'a narrow conception' of value added, but it was seen as the only practicable one in the short term.

Six types of 'index' methods and a comparative method for calculating value-added were tested in the project against actual data sets. The 'index' methods all arbitrarily attribute scores to the measures of input (entry qualification) and output (degree class) and calculate value-added by relating the two scores. They attempt to relate separate measures of entry and exit qualifications by making arbitrary assumptions about how hard it is for students to achieve a given exit qualification. The research claimed to show that 'all of the index methods, through the weightings they assign to entry and exit qualifications, are wrong about the nature of the relationship between the two. They all assume that it is more difficult to get a good degree with low entry qualifications than is in practice the case' (paragraph 7.1). As a result, the value-added scores they produce are biased in favour of courses with low A level and non-A level recruitment.

By contrast, the report claims, the comparative value-added (CVA) method maintains the distinction between measures of entry and exit by comparing degree results expected for students with particular entry qualifications with the actual degree results achieved. The expected degree class is derived from the national relationship between degree results and entry qualifications, therefore it is the expectation of a student with a particular qualification gaining a particular degree. The value added score of a course, a programme area, an institution or a sector, is a function of the difference between the degree results achieved and the results predicted from entry qualifications. The report claims there are two advantages of the CVA method:

> 'Firstly, it is not an arbitrary score, but is based on an empirically derived expected value. Therefore the claim that a particular course did better or worse than expected when compared to national data is likely to have a robust acceptability. Secondly, because the playing field has been levelled all institutions have an incentive to improve their value added scores whatever their current recruitment profile' (paragraph 3.7).

This claim overstates what the CVA method can achieve. Any estimate of the value-added in a course, programme area, institution or sector involves aggregation of the value-added of many individuals. It is thus sensitive to the weights used to measure exit attainments. Although the CVA approach eliminates the need for explicit weighting of input qualifications, by adopting national performance as a yardstick, it still requires an explicit set of weights for exit qualifications. Thus it assumes that the difference in value between a first and upper second is the same as that between an unclassified degree and a fail. Clearly this is contestable, and it demonstrates the impossibility of devising any system of value-added which is wholly free of arbitrary weights.

The CVA approach is similar to the improved method we shall see in Chapter 3.5 was adopted by the CVCP/UGC when devising a first destination PI. The main use for value-added proposed by the Morris Committee is to provide a macro PI to show at an inter-sectoral level that, 'relatively high performance in terms of 'value-added' is a distinctive characteristic of the PCFC sector, and of individual institutions within it.' Further uses recommended by the PCFC/CNAA Report include: PCFC should indicate to institutions that high CVA scores will be taken into account by Programme Committees in considering quality bids; PCFC should monitor national trends in subject and sector differences in value-added; PCFC, CNAA and institutions should all use CVA as part of their monitoring of access policies; and because of the contribution CVA will make to quality assurance, CNAA should encourage institutions to use CVA in their course monitoring and review processes. Furthermore, at the institutional level it could be very useful as part of quality assurance because the CVA method can calculate value-added for different kinds of entrant, even on the same course. Institutions already routinely examine data on entry qualifications and student performance as part of course monitoring and validation procedures. It is claimed that the value of these data to these procedures will be enhanced by use of the CVA method because:

> '(i) the CVA method can produce summary statistics of student performance that will be meaningful at academic board/ governors levels;
>
> (ii) it can also provide a very detailed breakdown of performance and the factors which have influenced it for use at the course committee level' (paragraph 7.5.3).

There are, however, several possible criticisms of the value-added approach as described. Firstly, some people question one of the basic assumptions made, namely that degree classifications are comparable between institutions and between sectors. Furthermore, if CVA was to be used by PACs when assessing quality bids, the danger of manipulation might increase despite the existence of external examiners. The project also showed how value-added was greater on some courses for females and for mature students. However, it was not suggested that such factors could be allowed for when calculating the expected value-added and then the CVA for one course when compared with another, and yet, the differences between courses at different institutions might be entirely accounted for by such factors, and thus reveal nothing about the relative quality of the courses. As we noted earlier, Johnes and Taylor (1987) developed their predicted degree results for each university by standardising for inter-university variations in a range of explanatory variables.

A fundamental objection is that the conception of value-added is too narrow. A much wider interpretation of the concept of value-added is being encouraged in UK higher education by, for example, the Enterprise Initiative. It is useful to examine the whole nature of the debate about value-added from a much wider perspective, and most of the examples come from the United States.

The concept of value-added is simple. We consider two individuals identical in every respect until the decision to enter higher education is taken. One goes on to take a degree of a given quality; the other does not. The value-added by the degree is the difference in the contributions made to the welfare of society by the two individuals. This definition of value-added in terms of social worth is necessarily broad. Education is of value to the individual in terms of the consumption benefits of undergoing it, the pecuniary advantages of increased earnings potential, and other benefits in terms of personal development. The benefits to society derive from having one more highly educated individual, which may be desirable in itself if society values education *per se*, and from any positive externality effects. An example of a positive externality of education often cited is that a well educated person may increase the productivity of a less well educated person, either by adopting more efficient methods of work, or by the less well educated person learning from the highly educated employee (see Le Grand and Robinson 1979).

The importance of the ability to measure value-added lies in the information which it could provide in respect of the relationship between inputs and outputs, ie the efficiency of the education process. The more efficient institutions produce more value-added at the same or a lower cost. In this sense the efficiency of one institution relative to any other can be crudely measured by the ratio of average value-added to average cost. The higher the ratio the more efficient the institution. Measuring value-added is also important because it should allow the nature of the returns to scale in teaching to be explored more fully. In order to be able to allocate resources efficiently information is required on how outputs change in response to marginal changes in inputs. At present we do not have a measure of the output of the teaching process and this might, in principle, be provided by the value-added measure. Egan even claims that a value-added testing programme can 'help determine if increments to undergraduate teaching budgets can generate increments to learning achievement of students, other things equal' and he suggests it could help with marginal funding decisions (p.35).

In practice, of course, it is impossible to realise the conception of value-added set out above. We lack the ability to perform a controlled experiment with two individuals, and the capacity to measure the benefits described above. Most attempts to implement the value-added approach do so by comparing the academic attainment of students entering the institution with their attainment on graduation; the assumption is that either all or a given proportion of the increase is associated with the educational process rather than due, say, to the passage of time. Compared with the simple output measure, this basic value-added method does try to 'correct' for differences in quality of student input.

In the USA Egan suggested that the instruments usually used in value-added measures were the SAT or ACT scores conventionally used to measure the academic ability or quality of students entering a HEI and the Graduate Record Examination (GRE) or similar tests conventionally used as measures of educational accomplishment at or near the time of exit of undergraduates from a HEI. Both sets of tests are expressed in percentiles and therefore to use them to show value-added poses a threat to the top HEIs which recruit their students from the top percentiles and therefore 'no display of net learning is possible in these cases because no dramatic percentile improvement is possible . . . the development of testing or assessment instruments, free of percentile ranking is essential if value-added testing and measurement is to become a dominant movement in higher education' (p.15/16). In the UK although there is room for debate about the extent to which A levels and degrees are norm referenced, similar fears might exist in the top ranking universities if the simple value-added approach was adopted.

An attempt to measure value-added on a concurrent basis has been made at the Northeast Missouri State University (NMSU). Taylor, T., (1985) describes the purpose of the value-added assessment at NMSU as to 'measure the gains in knowledge, skills and personal development within each individual'. He identifies two driving forces behind its introduction already noted. First, where the funding of universities in the USA has been based upon measures of throughput of students, the incentive for universities to do well against these quantitative measures has detracted from what should be an emphasis on quality. Second, there has been growing dissatisfaction with the traditional methods of assessing student performance and a greater public desire to measure the extent to which education results in an improvement in individuals in broader terms.

The NMSU programme grew from the modest beginnings of comparing students' results on the ACT entrance examination and those in a subsequent test after the second year. This was later extended to final year undergraduates, and now the NMSU attempts to measure a wide range of perspectives on value-added in a variety of different ways including 'Attitude surveys, interviews, objective standard tests, course taking patterns, subjective tests and extensive performance sampling' (Taylor, T. 1985). In addition, students are assessed prior to attending and after leaving university.

The diagnostic potential of the programme was illustrated at NMSU in 1979. Tests applied to business majors revealed that inadequate improvements had been made in the area of mathematics. Similar results were also indicated by tests applied to business graduates, by faculty experience in the classroom and by questionnaires given to students, the results of which indicated student perceptions of unpreparedness in mathematics. McClain et al (1986) argue that the fact that all of these tests indicate a weakness provides clear evidence of the existence of a problem.

As a result, curriculum committees met to discuss approaches which could be taken to improve the mathematical skills of their students and recommended that a stronger mathematics foundation be required for all four-year business majors. The recommendation became effective in 1979/80 with the result that in each of the subsequent years, test results showed improvement and questionnaire results indicated higher satisfaction amongst students with their mathematics preparedness. In addition, since the university internal budget allocation was closely tied to student outcomes, the improvements achieved translated into fiscal benefits. Thus McClain et al. maintain that the programme at NMSU makes it possible to diagnose a problem and offers incentives for its solution. In addition, the agency responsible for organising and implementing the changes was the faculty and not an external institution.

Taylor believes that there have been two important side effects of the introduction of the value-added programme. It has meant that the faculties within NMSU are now taking the view that 'students come first'. The emphasis has moved from attention to quantity to attention to both quantity and quality. Second, it has allowed NMSU to demonstrate to funding authorities and the general public that the education process is contributing value to individuals, thus allowing NMSU to demonstrate that resources spent on educating their students have been invested well.

One of the problems most often raised in connection with specific value-added assessment is that the procedure itself bestows no direct positive benefit on the student. The results of the test are used solely for the purpose of evaluating institutions or departments and, as such, the student has no particular incentive to do as well as possible. This may limit the extent to which such tests can elicit increases in skills.

Even if the tests do draw out accurate information on the particular aspect of personal development with which they are concerned, what weighting should be used to combine scores into a composite index? It has been noted that at NMSU various student characteristics are evaluated in several ways. Which components are most important? In order to compare scores across universities it is necessary for each university to agree to the same weighting system. If the purpose is to measure private benefits then the weights that are used should also be consistent with the valuation which students make of the differing components of private benefit.

Assuming that the value-added programme accurately reflects the private benefit derived from the education process, can we maintain that such measures accurately reflect social benefits from higher education? One of the problems of comparing the value of different degrees is that they have different social values. Different graduates are compensated by the market at varying rates and provide different social benefits. Does the same value-added score for different types of graduates imply the same social worth? If not we cannot infer relatively high social worth from a relatively high value-added score over different subjects.

There are also practical difficulties involved in measurement. In order validly to compare the scores from different institutions, it is necessary for tests to be standardised. As a result, rather than being a measure of quality, the value-added score becomes the definition of quality. Institutions, if they derive benefit from high value-added scores, have an incentive to reorganise their teaching practices to score well in value-added assessments. The familiar problem of a 'regression towards the mean' may occur, and after some time it may become difficult to discriminate between institutions on the basis of value-added scores. In the USA value-added has not been applied across institutions and there are other forms of multi-institutional and comparative measures.

Although value-added appeared in the earlier list of items given by Brinkman and Tester that could be used for inter-institutional comparison, McMillan (1988) argues:

> 'value-added education is tailored to the student characteristics and unique mission of each institution. This promotes the maintenance of diversity in higher education by encouraging varied assessments that avoid inappropriate inter-institutional comparisons' (p.19).

Egan showed that not only students but also policies, programmes and personnel would be evaluated using value-added. He therefore claimed that faculty members as well as institutional leaders would be expected to oppose externally imposed value-added programmes. The only way out of this dilemma would be if the faculty members themselves choose to use value-added measurements to advance the goals of undergraduate instruction which they have chosen as their primary goal' (p.23). If this could be done it would provide information for the consumers/students; re-establish and institutionalise undergraduate teaching as a primary institutional goal; and show the students the progress they were making. Furthermore publication of the results would maximise the 'internal incentives for effective undergraduate education by subjecting the HEI to external market and/or political rewards and punishments for effective and ineffective education' (p.26). For reasons similar to those developed in the previous section Egan believed that lecturers inevitably tend to devote more attention to research and postgraduate education than to undergraduate teaching and that 'HEIs have few or no incentives to adopt value-added measures' (p.51). A further practical difficulty with the operation of a concurrent value-added assessment is that it would be both time consuming and costly. Even if appropriate standard tests could be agreed, testing would have to be carried out at least twice in each institution for each student, or for a large random sample of students, for a 'before and after' measurement to be made. Whether the cost exceeds the benefit depends in part on how well value-added measures reflect the output of the education process. Research into a number of large research universities shows limited involvement in activities commonly associated with the assessment movement such as measures of value-added. It is argued that 'the logistical problems of testing and retesting using standardised exams prohibit any value-added analyses' (Ory and Parker 1989, p.384).

Some of the problems of measuring the wider interpretation of value-added have been mentioned here. However, research in this area is still in its infancy and by no means at a stage where we can say that value-added measures can or cannot be made operational at some level.

If we were able to measure value-added, the efficiency of institutions could be explored and the usefulness or otherwise of investment in higher education demonstrated. Additionally, we could examine the relationship between inputs and outputs at the margin and go some way towards estimating the optimal size of the institutions assessed. Yet, as we have seen, the measurement of value-added is not without difficulty. Even if reliable information can be derived from such tests, what relative weights should we apply to the aspects of personal development measured? Do measurements reflect social benefits? There are also practical difficulties. Once relevant and universal measures have been achieved the concurrent measurement of value-added would be very expensive and time consuming. Finally, the introduction of universal value-added measurement may, if institutions derive benefit from higher value-added scores, result in teaching practices being altered to prepare students to do well in such tests. Value-added measures may no longer measure what they were intended to measure.

Despite these difficulties, some authors feel that further studies in this area would be money well spent. However, as already noted, Astin (1982) points out 'such studies frequently take a long time to produce useful results, and the results are often so general that they are difficult for individual institutions to apply to their particular problems'. The result is that funds for such research, which would allow the usefulness of higher education to be tested, are not readily available.

3.3 Using Cost Measures as Performance Indicators

What Do Measures of Average Cost Mean?

Average cost per student or per graduate is a natural performance indicator. It combines measures of inputs and of outputs. It is available by cost centre in UFC statistics, and it lends itself naturally to comparative analysis by calculating the average cost per student in a discipline in one university and comparing it with a national average or average of similar institutions. In some ways, average cost per graduate is the more satisfactory variant because it is a true output measure rather than a process measure. In practice, however, average cost per student is more widely used. The two will diverge when there are differences in wastage rates between institutions. One particularly simple variant of the cost measure is the staff-student ratio. This measure ignores all inputs other than labour supplied by lecturers, and may therefore encourage inefficient substitution of other inputs - for example, equipment or secretarial and administrators' time - for inputs from lecturers. It also makes no distinction between teachers of different seniority and income levels. This, too, may lead to distorted measurement and distorted incentives. For instance, it may encourage inefficient substitution between lecturers' time and other inputs.

All average cost measures (whether expressed in monetary terms or in the simplified form of staff-student ratios) are subject to a number of difficulties in the measurement of both inputs and outputs. As far as inputs are concerned the allocation of an institution's costs to a particular department or cost centre raises many practical difficulties, and consistency of treatment must be attained if inferences are to be drawn from comparative data. It is also inappropriate to assume that all costs are teaching costs, or that teaching costs are the same proportion of costs in all universities. Some costs, such as the opportunity cost of lost research, are inherently difficult or impossible to measure.

There are problems, too, of measuring output. One of these is that of aggregating undergraduate, postgraduate taught and postgraduate research students into a single measure, and this is not attempted in the USA. Traditionally the weights adopted in the UK were chosen fairly arbitrarily, rather than based on an evaluation either of relative costs or of relative benefits. Moreover, universities often used for internal resource allocation purposes a different set of weights than those adopted by the UGC. We have already noted the case for adopting value-added as the measure of output rather than number of students graduating or receiving instruction. On this basis, even if entry standards were uniform across institutions there is still the question of whether output standards are identical - whether a degree in a given class is of uniform value across all institutions.

Uncertainty about output quality can lead to conflicting interpretations of a high cost per student. By one interpretation high unit cost (say a high staff-student ratio) may be taken as an indicator of a high quality educational process. If there were a direct relationship between the amount of time allocated to students and the quality of degree obtained, then higher staff-student ratios would be associated with higher quality output. However, we have no information on the quality of degrees and hence we are unable to investigate the relationship between teaching time and student quality. In this sense, the existence of a high staff-student ratio is not sufficient to indicate high quality.

The second interpretation leads to opposite conclusions. If degrees of the same grade are of the same quality, irrespective of the awarding institution, and if the value-added to an individual of obtaining a degree of the same class is the same for all institutions, then average cost may, in certain conditions, be used as an index of efficiency. However, the conditions required for such a conclusion to be valid for inter-university comparisons are fairly restrictive.

In order to draw straightforward inferences from cost-effective comparisons it is desirable, first, that different institutions have, or at least have access to, the same 'production technologies' and, secondly, that they face identical prices.

By a production technology we mean the ability to turn inputs into outputs, or, in other words, the ability to transform an individual without a degree into an individual with a degree. This also requires each department to have access to the technology and not be locked into a particular production process which may not be optimal; we must suppose that it can alter teaching intensity, equipment levels, and the like to the optimal level.

The latter condition requires that the cost of the same production process must be the same for different institutions, so that institutions are not disadvantaged by such factors as the inherited age structure of their staff, their location or differences in research potential. There are a number of reasons why these conditions are unlikely to hold.

Firstly, universities have inherited various 'structural differences' which do not allow them to operate at the optimum level. 'Structure' here means the nature of the technology available to the university. This will include the staff (which may be tenured) as well as buildings and teaching equipment - for example, computers. The availability of these resources is also intimately affected by funding policies. If the allocation is not correct some institutions may not be able to achieve their optimal output because they have insufficient resources to do so; ie they may be constrained to an output level which is below that at which they would achieve maximum efficiency.

Using average cost as a measure of comparative efficiency now becomes problematical. An institution with higher than average costs may find itself in this position for two reasons (here we assume that outputs of all institutions are of equivalent quality). Either it may be inefficient in using its resources, or it may be forced by circumstances outside its control to incur higher than average costs. If the funding body is concerned only with minimising unit costs, it may adopt the same policy in either case - of concentrating resources on low unit cost institutions. If it is concerned with other objectives as well - for example, ensuring a regional balance in higher education institutions or providing incentives for efficient use of given resources - it will be more inclined to concern itself with the explanation of higher unit costs.

Data on costs incurred will not be adequate for such purposes, although some progress might be made by identifying subsets of comparable institutions and using those as benchmarks to evaluate performance.

The second major problem is that of estimating the 'opportunity cost' of lost research - the cost implied by the value of research lost as a result of time devoted to teaching. This is not directly measured by costs per FTE, but it has an important bearing on the use of average cost as a measure of comparative cost effectiveness. Without measuring the opportunity cost of lost research we cannot say whether true average costs (including the opportunity cost of lost research) are different between departments. Thus taking a low average cost to imply cost effectiveness may be misleading since the low (measured) average cost may be associated with a high opportunity cost of lost research. This kind of cost, which depends on the potential research productivity of a department or institution, cannot be established by cost allocation procedures of the kind set out in the Clayton Report (1987).

Why should the opportunity cost of lost research differ between departments? Perhaps a more appropriate question is: why should the implied costs of lost research be the same? Departments differ in research capabilities; otherwise we should not try to rank them. The opportunity cost associated with lost research in a 'good' research department is, therefore, likely to be higher than an equivalent time lost in a 'bad' research department. However, we must be careful in interpreting the relationship since good research departments may have more staff, each of whom devotes a smaller proportion of total time to teaching. It is possible, therefore, that the implied cost associated with a good department may be lower depending on the extent to which there are economies of scale in teaching. What is clear is that without some measurement of the implied cost of lost research the interpretation of average cost as a performance indicator will be ambiguous. Yet such measurements are not possible with even approximate accuracy.

Thirdly, as we have noted, the cost-effectiveness of a cost centre or department is also going to depend directly upon the quality of the inputs to the production of degrees, ie student quality. If different universities have varying qualities of student demand then average cost may vary for reasons unrelated to the cost-effectiveness of the cost centres.

The relationship here is again unclear. First of all, we need to ask whether students of higher quality benefit more or less from a given level of teaching than students of a lower quality. If there is no difference, variations in the quality of student demand for places do not affect average cost. This is because, other things being equal, the optimal amount of teaching input is uniform across departments, regardless of variations in student quality. In this case, average cost may well be a useful indicator of cost-effectiveness. However, if the quality of students directly affects the productivity of teaching resources this is no longer the case.

It was argued earlier that, because we are unable to measure the quality of degrees, the best we can hope to obtain from using average teaching costs is some measure of comparative efficiency. Departments with lower average teaching costs are producing degrees (of a uniform quality) more cost-effectively. However, a fair comparison requires not only that the quality of output is uniform, but also that each department has available, or at least access to, the same production technology and faces the same prices. This may not be the case; differences among cost centres in structure, in the opportunity cost of lost research, and in the quality of student input mean that average teaching cost may vary between departments without implying anything about relative cost effectiveness. Unless the effects of these differences can be removed from average teaching costs, differences in average teaching costs may simply indicate that departments are doing the best they can subject to their available resources. This may still leave a role for more disaggregated cost per student data as triggers of questions to be asked. For instance, if materials cost per student in one chemistry department are twice as high as the national average, it is reasonable to wonder why that state of affairs has arisen. Even at the level of total cost per student, the same sort of issues are raised.

In their second (1987) statement, the CVCP/UGC Working Group, as we saw in Chapter 2, note the criticism that their 1986 list of proposed PIs gave too much attention to inputs and too little to outputs. They also note the concern 'that due consideration and weight should be given to local or regional factors, be they geographical, structural or economic, especially in inter-university comparisons'. Nevertheless, shortage of data has meant that even in 1990 the Management Statistics and Performance Indicators are overwhelmingly related in one way or another to costs.

Clearly what is lacking is an adequate data set which would enable us to unravel the inter-relations between properly measured inputs into and properly measured outputs of the teaching process. If such a data set were available, it would be possible to estimate the same kind of statistical cost functions as have been estimated in other contexts. This approach would also have the considerable advantage of yielding estimates not only of average cost but also of marginal cost. One or two attempts of this kind have been made (see, for instance, Osborne 1989). But even with available data, there is clearly scope for more analysis of this kind. A good example is provided by Jill Johnes' (1990a) study of differences in unit cost among UK universities, which shows that two-thirds of the variation is accounted for by different disciplinary mixes, and a further one-seventh by the staff-student ratio and the student composition. But the remainder is unexplained and the author draws attention to the need for better output measures before conclusions about efficiency can be drawn.

3.4 Wastage and Completion Rates

The problems associated with linking PIs with the objectives of higher education and ensuring that they are used properly by management are particularly acute in the case of wastage rates. The CVCP/UGC Working Group in their 1986 report cited undergraduate wastage rates as an example when referring to 'limitations to [the] use of performance indicators and dangers in an unsophisticated or thoughtless reliance on the signposts that they provide'. The Working Group pointed out that whilst the undergraduate wastage rate could be useful as a means of monitoring the success of an institution in the output of graduates and as a reflection of the quality of teaching, the maintenance of academic standards might mean that a certain level of wastage was unavoidable. At the level of postgraduate and research degrees, the problems are rather different.

The issue became more evident when the Secretary of State made it clear that he wished to see an increase in access to higher education (Baker 1986 and 1987) and the CVCP issued a circular calling for wider access. The chairman of the UGC made it clear to universities that they would not be putting themselves at a disadvantage by 'lowering their admission standards for mathematics and physics courses in order to admit more students who are considering eventually becoming school teachers' (Swinnerton-Dyer 1986). The policies of widening access to higher education will be put in jeopardy if, as a result of taking more 'higher risk' students, institutions have a higher wastage rate for which they are penalised. There are further methodological problems with this superficially straightforward PI. In the ancient Scottish universities and some of the colleges of the University of Wales, transfer between courses is relatively common and therefore 'wastage' at departmental level does not have the same meaning as elsewhere. This would militate against their application at the departmental level in such circumstances. There are also problems with ascribing wastage to a department in the case of multidisciplinary courses. Both the Green Paper (DES 1985) and Cullen (1987) referred to the absence of accurate data on non-completion rates (although they refer to the public sector and not the universities); however, this problem is being remedied.

Despite the difficulties, the Working Group suggested in 1986 that this PI could be adopted in the near future. The 1987 White Paper (DES 1987) also supported the use of non-completion rates as an indicator of the quality of teaching. It would be of considerable use for planning purposes, especially on courses such as teacher training where an attempt is made at planning labour supply, as well as in monitoring the success of an institution in producing graduates. Its value in revealing possible problems within the institution could be great provided it were used sensitively and in conjunction with other indicators such as entry standards, cost per student and research output. For example, an institution which combined high wastage rates with high entry standards, high costs and a low publication rate could be deemed to have problems. At the very least a high wastage rate suggests the need for an investigation into its causes. Some people would argue that even if the high level is a result of the high standards on the course, the institution could still be criticised for poor initial selection. Possibly it would be helpful here to distinguish between compulsory and voluntary wastage. There might be different reasons for each and, in the case of the latter, possibly the PI could be formulated to incorporate an evaluation of the procedures for counselling students. It is worth noting that in the USA retention and drop-out rates are viewed as important indicators of the quality of teaching or of a particular programme.

The importance of careful handling of this PI is underlined by the regression analysis undertaken by Johnes and Taylor (1989). They show that a large proportion of the inter-university variation in the non-completion rate can be explained by three factors: the ability of each university's entrants (as reflected by A-level score); the subject mix; and the proportion of each university's students accommodated in a hall of residence. This raises serious doubts about the validity of using non-completion rates as a PI of teaching. Johnes and Taylor suggest that for such comparisons to be much use 'each university's non-completion rate would first need to be 'corrected' for at least some of the factors responsible for causing inter-university disparities' (p.224). Johnes and Taylor (1991) also show that many non-completers went on to get degrees elsewhere, though as a group, non-completers earned less than graduates.

The Morris Report recommended that an Index of Output Costs should be developed as one of the macro PIs to be used by the PCFC. It should be constructed by multiplying the Index of Revenue Resource by the reciprocal of the Course Completion Index. If there were then a fall in the Index of Revenue Resource, accompanied by a fall in course completion rates, there might be no improvement in the Index of Output Costs.

The first suite of PIs produced in 1987 by the CVCP/UGC did not include an indicator of wastage rate. In the improved 1988 list, however, an indicator of undergraduate success was introduced. The conventional indicator of 'wastage' or 'drop out' rate was eschewed and instead the main time spent by students in acquiring a degree is considered. The concept of 'terms of attendance' per success has been developed and is also expressed as the number of years a student studies as a percentage of the length of undergraduate course. In the first year in which it was used, the way in which this PI was reported in *The Times* led to angry letters of protest. League tables were produced by the paper showing, in seven subjects, the most successful universities in terms of the examination success rate. Letters pointed out that some of the universities appearing very high in the tables had achieved their position on the basis of graduating all of a very small number of students on the particular courses. Page, Chairman of the CVCP/UGC Committee, declared that the article 'exhibits in stark fashion precisely the dangers I warned against in that report: namely, the league tables will always be misleading, particularly when they are based on one only of the many sets of statistics' (*The Times*, 8 October 1988).

At the postgraduate level the CVCP/UGC Working Group has proposed a (non) submission rate for doctorates and other research degrees as the graduate equivalent of the undergraduate wastage rate. This has not yet been adopted into their suite of indicators. Submission rates have been used for many years by the Research Councils to help determine their allocation of studentships. Both the Science and Engineering Research Council (SERC) and the Economic and Social research Council (ESRC) have in recent years set an optimum length of four years full time, sponsored, research for a PhD; students who have not submitted their thesis within that period do not receive further financial support. The ESRC developed its use of this PI further, putting a greater onus on the institution training the student to exact submission of a thesis within the four year period. Amidst strong protests, institutions with ESRC-sponsored students which achieved a four year submission rate of less than 25% over a three year period were blacklisted: students are not permitted to take their studentship awards to those institutions. The ratio was raised to 35%, then to 40%, and is now 50% and will have to get up to 70% to match that of other research councils. Refinements were introduced to allow institutions to put forward selected departments for recognition and so overcome the problem that some institutional blacklistings resulted from a single department with very low completion rates. It has now been recognised that the submission rate measures not only student input but also the institution's admission policy, the quality of its supervisory practices and the level of research activity within its departments. This PI therefore relates to more than just the teaching function.

The outcry over the ESRC's code of practice does, however, indicate that the use of the PI is not without problems. The criticisms of the policy have continued with a recent letter to the *Times Higher Education Supplement* claiming of 'the ESRC's unseen unvalidated measure of departmental performance . . . [that] . . . if reasoning of the type justifying blacklisting was found in one's PhD . . . we would be immediately failed' (23 February 1990). Amongst the social sciences departments blacklisted under the 25% rule were those at established, well-regarded research centres such as University College London, Bath, Bristol and Sussex. Some have now had the sanction removed but more recent universities to be sanctioned include Cambridge. Many of the larger institutions have argued that the very size of their research student population has worked against them. Others have argued more generally against the use of wastage rates as a performance indicator on the grounds that success in training postgraduates leads to wastage: students are attracted to highly paid jobs in industry before they can complete their degrees. This is a particular problem in areas such as electrical engineering and computer science and it is not clear how it can be satisfactorily incorporated in a PI. SERC, however, have used the PI as a 'tin-opener', in the terminology of Klein and Carter (1988), to raise questions about the appropriateness of the current nature of PhDs in engineering.

As with undergraduate wastage rates, the data on submission rates for research degrees require careful analysis before they can be used for inter-institutional comparisons (the use for which the CVCP/UGC 1986 Working Group recommended them). The Working Group recommended that initially only full time research students should be surveyed. This group is not large in many institutions, and the results can be distorted by individual cases. The ESRC has attempted to minimise the distortions caused by small samples by using a rolling three year average on which to calculate submission rates. But this, too, is open to problems and several institutions have appealed against blacklisting on this historic basis. One of the reasons for not extending the sample to include part time students is the problem of annotating reasons for withdrawal. The University Statistical Record (USR) identifies only six: academic, health, death, financial, unspecified or award. These make no allowance for the success of students in obtaining more gainful employment. The CVCP is actively researching 'legitimate reasons' for failure to submit, but such adjustments create further problems of measurement and classification.

The use of submission rates as a performance indicator may have long term consequences for the nature of postgraduate student research in this country. If the PI becomes a definition of success rather than one of several measures, it could lead to distortion of the doctoral system; students would be admitted to undertake narrow, superficial or barely original research assured of completion within four years. There seems to be consensus that the majority of full time students should submit a PhD within four years, but it is not proven whether past submission rates in all areas would justify this. The emphasis on submission rather than completion or award must also be noted, as this criterion could be open to abuse. The CVCP/UGC technical committee explained in 1987 that submission rates for research degrees could not be included among the indicators proposed for immediate use because the data examined 'showed that there was no centrally co-ordinated or reliable data base available'.

The sanctions policy, and use of the PI as a 'dial' in the terminology of Klein and Carter, are very important to the ESRC. The policy has dramatically increased the submissions rate of social science PhDs. Furthermore, the Chairman of the ESRC has expressed the fear that the current number of research studentships, would not be sufficient to produce a sustainable social science community in the 1990s. To gain more money to increase the number of studentships, particularly in the light of critical comments from the House of Commons Public Accounts Committee, it would be necessary to increase the PhD submissions rate still further to convince people that the ESRC was serious about improving training: 'the ESRC cannot make a credible case for additional resources unless this crucial 'performance indicator' improves' (Newby, *Times Higher Education Supplement*, 30 March 1990). It is clear that PhD submission rate is used as a PI for research councils as well as for universities. There is a debate about the appropriateness of using this indicator in various ways at a number of different levels in the higher education/ research system (Cave and Hanney 1990).

The use of wastage rates as a performance indicator involves the central problem we have identified before - that of quality control. Any institution has the theoretical capacity to influence its own wastage or completion rate by the standards it imposes. Departments are constrained from doing so both by a sense of academic and professional responsibility and by the system of accreditation and the external examining of undergraduate and postgraduate degrees and research theses. Nonetheless, if wastage rates were adopted as a major PI the pressures to distort academic judgement would become more severe. A particular advantage of distinguishing between compulsory and voluntary wastage would be that the latter would be much less vulnerable to such strategic action by the Department. In the case of postgraduate degrees there is the additional problem that - depending on employment opportunities - it may be neither individually nor socially efficient for a student to complete.

3.5 Employment and First Destinations

The extent to which higher education makes students more employable in the labour market is obviously and legitimately a matter of great concern to governments, institutions, employers and the students themselves. It is not surprising, therefore, that the destinations to which higher education leads have been used as an indicator of the effectiveness of institutions of undergraduate education in articles in the serious press. They are also listed in the CVCP/UGC table of indicators. The Department of Employment and the DES have been keen to publicise first destination statistics (FDS) in order better to inform intending graduates about their career prospects (DES and DE 1985). They are also regarded as an important indicator in the USA (Miller 1986).

In the United Kingdom, careful studies of first destinations have been undertaken by Johnes, J., and Taylor, J., at Lancaster University (see, for example, Taylor, J. 1985; Johnes and Taylor, J. 1989a). These involve collection of employment data by subject or subject group in each university and the establishment of an overall 'employability' rate which takes account of differences among institutions in the composition of output. Such a correction eliminates approximately three-quarters of differences among universities. Of the remainder, the greatest contribution to an explanation was made by the type of university and its age, recruiting practices of employees, and the rate of unemployment where the university is located. About 10% of the variation remains unexplained.

Recent research, however, challenges the reliability of figures compiled too soon after graduation. Two recent studies address the point directly.

Brennan and McGeevor (1988) in their survey of CNAA graduates at work conclude that the high volume of job changes during the three years after graduation suggests that the use of first destination statistics to imply anything more than first destinations can be misleading. The year immediately after graduation has an important but very different role to play for different kinds of graduates in making the transition into employment. During the first three years of graduate employment a large amount of change takes place. Fifty eight per cent of CNAA graduates had two jobs or more during this period. 43% changed their employment status between 1983 and 1985. In autumn 1985, 18% were actively looking for a different kind of job.

These figures suggest a number of things. The first is that graduates are able to change jobs, that is to say, the labour market provides opportunities for them to do so. Secondly, many graduates want to change jobs. Some job changes may be enforced but in the main they are the result of graduates looking for something better. In the first year after graduation, many graduates are taking postgraduate courses or clearly temporary jobs. However, even after the third year after graduation, 23% changed the type of work they were doing.

On these grounds, Brennan and McGeevor suggest that 'the use of these statistics to imply more than first destinations may be extremely dangerous'. 'If higher education policy is going to continue its emphasis on outcomes, then better measures of them than are currently available will need to be found.'

There are other criticisms of their use. The Association of Graduate Careers Advisory Services (AGCAS), which annually produces its own guide (*What Do Graduates Do?*), has been critical of the approach adopted by the Department of Employment. It claims that insufficient attention has been drawn to variations between occupations in career paths towards permanent employment. Some careers require further periods of full time study after graduation; others, such as social work and graphic design, are typified by periods of short term employment in the early stages (Porrer 1984.) Among the questions asked about FDS is that of their reliability as indicators of long term prospects because they are collected relatively soon after graduation during a transitional period for many who have never held a permanent job before. It has been suggested that a more accurate picture of graduate unemployment might be given by calculating on a base figure which includes or excludes those who entered full time study soon after graduation.

Boys and Kirkland (1988) differ somewhat in their conclusions from Brennan and McGeevor. Using a cohort sample of 1,500 people graduating in 1982, they showed that a substantial proportion of those unemployed six months after graduation had experienced considerable difficulty in finding any job. Unemployment rates among graduates fell dramatically over the three years covered in the Brunel report; very few of those unemployed in 1982 were unemployed in 1985. Nevertheless, over one third of those unemployed, or not undertaking further study or without a permanent job arranged in December 1982, had experienced periods of unemployment totalling one year or more. They also tended to rate their career opportunities lower than other groups.

Boys concludes that first destination statistics do indicate difficulties in the labour market in the short term. They are also modest predictors of success in the labour market over the longer term. However, this interpretation is more controversial. The only satisfactory approach is to undertake long term employment studies, but the cost of doing so, on a level sufficiently large to permit inter-institutional comparisons, is likely to be prohibitive. This is implicitly accepted in the CVCP/UGC's second statement (1987) where, as we have seen, employment after six months, for which the data are already collected, was inserted instead of employment after 12 months and five years, which appeared in the first statement.

Further work, however, was carried out on this indicator and in 1988 these indicators were reformulated to take account of the difference in unemployment rates in different subjects as revealed by Taylor. Therefore indicator E42 on Table 2 was calculated and it is the number predicted to be unemployed, or in short term employment, if the national proportions for each subject were applied to the number of graduates in each subject included in the total number of graduates from a university whose destinations are known (indicator E40). Indicator E43 shows the excess or deficit of the expected value over the actual value of graduates unemployed or in short term employment. Indicator E44 shows the excess or deficit expressed as a percentage of those in indicator 40 so that a negative figure indicates more than the predicted proportion of unemployed or in short term employment and a positive figure less than predicted.

Taylor and Johnes (1989) also show that graduates who were unemployed six months after graduation did have poorer long term career prospects but that there was only limited correlation between the subjects with the lowest rates of unemployment after six months and those with the lowest rates of average salary after six years. It can thus be argued that this PI could be used more satisfactorily to compare universities than to compare subjects. The PCFC Report recommended that the AGCAS be invited to suggest how best to conduct an employment profile making use of 'First Destinations' and similar information. It was also claimed that as part of client satisfaction, not only should student feedback be used but also that of the employers.

Both in the UK and in Australia the employment rate of postgraduates has been proposed as a PI of research training.

3.6 Entry Standards

The potentially ambiguous place of entry standards in relation to value-added has already been noted as has the original exclusion, and subsequent inclusion, of entry-standards in the CVCP/UGC suite of PIs. There has been debate about the extent to which entry standards could be seen as a PI of the quality of teaching with high entry standards reflecting high demand from applicants for a placc at a department or HEI with a reputation for good teaching. Such considerations are not thought, however, to figure prominently in the minds of the majority of applicants.

This indicator illustrates a number of points about the importance of relating PIs to objectives. If the widening of access to HEIs and increasing the age participation rate are important objectives, then a stress on high entry scores could cause some difficulties. A recent report from the Training Agency on widening admissions to HE recommended that 'funding bodies (and especially the UFC) should adopt performance indicators to measure and reward HEIs' success in recruiting - and successful graduating - applicants with lower A-level scores and those with non-traditional qualifications' (Fulton and Ellwood 1989).

3.7 Student and Peer Review

Student review of teaching is much more frequently practised and more highly developed in the USA than in the UK. Using questionnaires to record students' judgements of their courses is generally the most favoured method of obtaining their opinions and the technique developed in the USA in the 1930s (Winter Hebron 1984). In replies from 39 institutions to the IMHE survey, 'student evaluation of teaching' was cited as a PI nine times - although not by any of the nine UK universities in the survey. Student evaluation of teaching is the most direct way in which teaching can be evaluated. Of the types of peer review, only classroom observation is as direct. Various aspects of peer review of departments, as described by the 1986 CVCP/UGC Working Party report, 'are hidden in others of the proposed performance indicators'. Some of the ways in which student and peer review of teaching may be conducted are considered in this section. There is, however, concern about what is actually being assessed and about technical problems which will be particularly difficult to overcome if student and peer review of teaching are to be built into a national system of PIs. It might be better to develop a more indirect system in which the PI is the extent to which teaching is assessed and the results used in a formative way to improve the teaching. It is also necessary to consider how a review of this type, which essentially operates at the level of the individual, can be aggregated over a department.

Student questionnaires in the 1930s in America developed at the same time as the rise of marketing studies and 'it is not surprising, therefore, that many of the earlier questionnaires were conducted along very similar lines to market research studies, and that this influence still persists' (Winter Hebron 1984). Linking with the consumerist approach to higher education in America noted in previous sections, some of these questionnaires tended to be essentially measures of student satisfaction with courses.

A second kind of instrument developed in America invites students to rate either what the instructor did or how frequently he or she did it. These instruments have been described by Winter Hebron as 'behaviourally referenced' systems, and an example is Instructional Development by Evaluation and Assessment (IDEA) developed at Kansas University. It is concerned with student perceptions of instructor behaviour and the progress made on a course towards agreed course objectives. Good teaching has thus been defined as instructor behaviour that relates to increased student perceptions of progress. The system concentrates on those things that students may properly be said to know about the teaching they receive. The system is then built upon the following:

(1) It asks the teacher to specify his key objectives from a given list.

(2) It records what students know about that teacher as responses on a five point scale.

(3) It compares the means and distributions of these scores with a nationally acquired data base, and prints out comparisons.

(4) For each behaviour and objective, a closeness of connection is calculated for the data base. This closeness is expressed in terms of the extent to which the variables seem to vary together in the same or in opposite directions.

(5) The system points out which of the teacher's low performance scores are most closely related to low scores on objectives.

(6) The data base is then itself updated by incorporating the individual teacher's performance scores.

Winter Hebron (1984) claims that 'The system does not, in itself, suggest specific corrective action to change the scores to which it points: it leaves that final self-corrective task to the individual teacher or his educational development consultant. But it does produce data which are readily understood, and which can be easily used to propose self-corrective changes in teaching strategy.'

According to Miller (1986) the standard of student questionnaires used in America is improving. Cook (1989) recently suggested that student ratings have provided the bulk of the data used in the United States in evaluating college teaching and, in their survey of large research institutions, Ory and Parker found that approximately 75% 'collect student ratings of instruction which provide an indicator of instructional quality' (p.31). Several years ago, according to Moses (1989), Australia was 10 to 15 years behind the USA in this field but ahead of the UK. They are increasingly being used in Australia (Moses 1986) and it is noted later how the introduction of a PI scheme has led to technical developments. Elton (1984) describes an Australian scheme in which appraisal forms are completed by peers and students; it is similar to many used in the USA. The student questionnaire requests students to rank their teachers on a five point scale for: organisation, feedback, knowledge of subject material, communication, responsiveness, comparison with other teachers.

Feedback from students has been used for a number of years in the evaluation of some higher education courses and teaching in the UK, (for example, at Newcastle Polytechnic (Torode 1980)) and the standard student feedback questionnaire is 'the most common form of evaluation technique employed by and recommended to lecturers' (Mathias and Rutherford 1982). There are also procedures which combine individual consultation with the use of student questionnaires (Bradbury and Ramsden 1975.) A UFC funded scheme for assessing teaching is being developed at Liverpool University involving student, peer and self-appraisal (*Times Higher Education Supplement*, 25 March 1990).

The 1986 CVCP/UGC report advocated the development of a system of individual teaching appraisal in all institutions. It continued, 'we would see the use of student questionnaires on the content and presentation of courses as an important part of this analysis'. In its White Paper (DES 1987) the government welcomed the CVCP's plans to publish guidelines for performance appraisal of academic staff and also argued that feedback from students should be used.

Winter Hebron has developed and adapted IDEA for use in Britain. His Assessment for Instructional Development (AID) scheme has been constructed using a data base drawn from six British universities and six polytechnics. It is focussed on the discipline-area into which the users' teaching falls and different versions exist for different major groupings of subjects. Student opinions can also often be gathered less formally. As Talbot and Bordage (1986) show, discussions with students can be systematically organised into highly structured 'directed small group discussions'.

Reviews of teaching can also be undertaken by peers. Although the 1986 CVCP/UGC list included peer review and cited UGC Sub-Committees as examples of peer review already being practised, it did not make it clear whether it is to be a PI of research, teaching or both, and it was omitted from the 1987 list. There are, however, cases where peer review of teaching has been attempted.

We have already noted the Australian example cited by Elton but here peers not only assess colleagues' teaching but also their scholarship and leadership. There are also schemes whereby the students' assessment is tested against peer assessments. This is done, for instance, in the Solmon and Astin study cited in Chapter 2. In the USA the regional accreditation procedures are largely carried out by peer review (Kells 1986). Miller includes several items that could be considered review by peers in his list given earlier of sources of information considered in evaluating faculty teaching performance. Feldman (1989) and Jordan (1989) analyse the large number of categories of people whose opinion can be sought about the quality of teaching. They include: students, faculty, alumni, administrators, employers, external observers. Feldman (1988) also reviewed over a hundred different articles on student review of teachers and showed that at least 22 different dimensions of instruction could be commented on.

An ambitious scheme at Birmingham University involved collaboration among lecturers to evaluate each other's courses. Teachers provided reciprocal evaluations and used a flexible combination of evaluation procedures designed to illuminate the characteristic features of each particular course (Mathias and Rutherford 1982). This was one of the few early British applications. At the level of 'reputational rankings' the major review of teaching conducted in the UK has been that of the *Times Higher Education Supplement* which asked heads of departments, amongst other questions, 'Which, in your view, are the five best departments in British Higher Education in your subject, bearing in mind mainly the quality of their teaching of undergraduate students' (*Times Higher Education Supplement*, 24 July 1987). This procedure is discussed further below in relation to research. It is doubtful, however, that heads of departments are in a good position to form judgements about teaching performance in other institutions.

Miller believes there are questions to which students, based on their observation of a teacher's performance, can give valid and reliable answers. Students, he claims, 'are the best judges of (a) teaching methods (pedagogy); (b) fairness, which primarily concerns testing; (c) interest in me; (d) interest in the subject; and (e) global questions such as 'How would you rate this teacher in comparison with all others that you have had thus far?'

He similarly suggests that two questions - (a) course organisation, and (b) course workload - can be asked of both students and colleagues. There are further questions that colleagues are best able to answer. These are: (a) the teacher's mastery of content; (b) selection of content; (c) relevance of content to the continuity of the course sequence; and (d) the relevance and quality of the course syllabus and related materials.

Partly as a result of court cases, Miller suggests that the quality and equity of faculty education in America have improved. There are now evaluation systems that include items such as the weighting to be given to the various evaluative components (1987a).

Having considered a range of techniques for student and peer review of teaching it is now important to analyse what they are valid indicators of and how they could be used. In 1986 the CVCP/UGC Working Party suggested that peer review could be used for comparisons between some cost centres in different institutions and possibly also apply across the binary line.

Student feedback on teaching is a direct evaluation of teaching and Fox (1984) argues that it is important 'to evaluate the teaching activities directly and not be misled into assuming that good learning (as demonstrated in examinations) necessarily reflects good teaching'.

Two divergent views emerge in the debate over the proper use of student ratings to evaluate teaching. The multi-dimensional view of evaluation, of which Marsh (1987) is a leading advocate, and the uni-dimensional approach backed by Abrami (1989). Marsh suggests that because teaching is multifaceted, student ratings should not be summarised by a response to a single item or an unweighted average response to many items. Instead, evaluations of teaching for summative or formative purposes should be based on factor scores from his Student's Evaluations of Educational Quality which uses nine dimensions. For summative purposes Abrami favours the use of several global rating items (for example, how would you rate this instructor in overall ability?) or a carefully weighted average of rating factors in lieu of separate factor scores. Similar issues have been analysed in New Zealand (Clift et al).

The study by Feldman (1989) of the various groups who judge the instructional effectiveness of college teachers revealed that the strongest cases of relative and absolute similarity in ratings are when ratings by current students are compared either with those by the teacher's colleagues or with administrators. Such findings correlate well with a review of articles about student ratings of their teaching. Murray (1984) gathered considerable evidence from North America and concluded that:

(a) the ratings of a given instructor are reasonably stable;

(b) student ratings correlate reasonably well with ratings made by others;

(c) there is a small but significant correlation with factors such as class size, and severity of gradings;

(d) there is a moderate positive correlation between student ratings of teaching and objective measures of student achievement.

This suggests that student ratings are sufficiently reliable and valid to justify their use as diagnostic feedback to the instructor and as one of several sources of information for such administrative decisions as faculty salary, retention, tenure and promotion (Murray 1984). The author cites evidence showing that teachers receiving favourable ratings from students promote higher levels of student achievements on objective tests than teachers receiving less favourable ratings. This suggests some correlation between high quality processes and high quality outputs. He goes on to suggest that some of the problems with making evaluations by students acceptable to lecturers in different departments, and yet also universally applicable (which is important for any PI), could be overcome by adopting a two level evaluation instrument which includes core items used in all departments together with optional items developed by individual departments and/or faculty members.

The points noted above go to the heart of the case against using peer, and especially student, reviews of teaching as PIs - they are not universally applicable. In 1986 the CVCP/UGC Working Party suggested, however, that the CVCP should issue notes of guidance on the appraisal of teachers so that the system should be as uniform as possible. Considerable work has since been devoted to this.

Many researchers have referred to the difficulties of using student judgement as a quantifiable PI for use in comparing departments or institutions as opposed to being used formatively in staff development. In 1989 Selmes reviewed various types of evaluation of teaching - by superiors, students, peers and outsiders - and considered the extent to which they were used in the UK. Although staff appraisal is now required in UK universities many were still in the process of implementing such schemes and 'little direct observation of teaching is involved' (p.169). Student questionnaires of teaching are not common and where they occur 'participation is voluntary and no systematic use of the data is made by administrators' (p.169). Evidence from peers is collected much less systematically in the UK than in North America but there is considerable evaluation by outsiders in the UK - the HMI, the CNAA and to some extent external examiners. Selmes believes that 'it may be inappropriate to try to devise a system which subjects all individuals to the same standardised process' (p.176).

A proposal contained in the Morris Report on performance indicators for the PCFC concerns the use of HMI quality profile and BTEC moderator profiles as performance indicators. The use of these profiles will be significant inasmuch as they would involve taking essentially qualitative judgements and converting them into indicators used at the sector level.

The HMI quality profile would use HMI's data base of current inspection reports as the basis for an indicator at sector level of the proportion of work both in each PCFC programme area and overall which falls within each of the five broad quality descriptors used by HMI. The BTEC moderator profile would be based on the system of twice yearly course ratings and external moderators. As with the HMI profile, the change over time in the shape of the corresponding quality distribution would provide a key indicator of the health of the significant part of total course provision in institutions. The profile might be constructed on a sample basis. The HMI descriptors range from '(a) generally good, or with some outstanding features or with many good features' to '(e) many shortcomings, generally poor' (Morris 1990).

Once again higher education in the UK is faced with the problem of attempting to develop and use a PI that might have policy implications and yet do so in a field where there is not much domestic research. Drew and Karpf claim that 'it is very difficult, if not impossible, currently to compare the quality of teaching in different schools'. Winter Hebron argues that in his AID scheme the criteria used are specific to the user's own teaching objectives and 'it cannot easily be used in a bureaucratic manner for overall accountability checking'. Mathias and Rutherford maintain that questionnaires are blind to contextual factors and it is difficult to see how either their schemes or that of Talbot and Bordage could be built into a PI. Elton (1984) develops a model for the evaluation of teaching based on his view that although useful checklists for good teaching can be compiled, it is neither possible nor desirable to establish general criteria against which an individual's performance can be assessed. He later notes (1987) that a framework similar to that applied in evaluation of research could be extended to teaching and suggests that 'student satisfaction with the teaching they receive' could be one of the PIs built into a model for determining the funding that each university should receive. However, he did not actually advocate such an approach or explain how the assessments of individual teachers could be built, in any meaningful way, into a model of PIs for an institution.

In their review of student ratings Dowell and Neal (1982) suggest that, because student characteristics are an important potential moderator of validity, local validation of the rating instruments should be conducted and evidence obtained that validity is reasonable before an instrument is used for policy decisions. Even then, the numerous biases and potential moderators documented in the literature 'suggest that different norms and different estimates of validity may be appropriate for different departments, course levels, and course types'.

For the reasons given above teachers are often suspicious of evaluations of their teaching. The application of prescriptive pressure, such as the attempt by the National Prices and Incomes Board of the 1960s to reward excellent or exacting teaching financially, can provoke significant resistance.

Rather in contradiction to Murray, Dowell and Neal show that some of the correlations between teaching assessment and student performance are not strong, and this raises doubts about what is actually being measured if the assessment of teaching is not well correlated with learning. Winter Hebron argues that traditional student questionnaires lack any way of establishing the validity of what they are measuring in terms of student learning and points to some research suggesting that 'their results may be too inconsistent in this area to be valid performance indications at all'. Rhodes and Rumery (1980) adopt a similar view.

The 1986 Working Group was criticised for separating staff appraisal from staff development in a way that, it is claimed, Jarratt had not intended (Wright 1987). The Working Group also suggested that the cost of carrying out full scale peer reviews limited the extent to which they can be used, not surprisingly, and it was not considered for inclusion in the initial list of PIs for use in 1987. Although some of the major reputational rankings in the USA have asked questions relating to teaching as well as research, Solmon and Astin report the difficulties involved in getting proper reputational rankings about teaching because academics tend not to know about the quality of teaching in other institutions. Further disadvantages with using peer review as a PI are discussed in Chapter 4.5.

The pressure on universities to pay greater attention to assessing the quality of teaching was noted earlier. The Audit Unit being established following the report from the Sutherland Standing Group will send an audit team to each university about every two years. The checklist given in Table 3 shows that much greater attention will have to be paid to assessing the quality of teaching. How many of the activities on the checklist could be turned into PIs is doubtful. However, one way in which student and/or peer assessment of teaching could be used to develop PIs useful for comparisons between institutions and between departments has been suggested in America by Astin and by the Tennessee scheme (see Chapter 2.2) and in Britain by Elton. It would be possible to quantify the extent to which mechanisms for student and/or peer assessment existed and were used in non-threatening formative ways to encourage staff development. Elton suggests that 'the very fact that a teacher uses them (student feedback forms) ought therefore to be counted as evidence for teacher assessment' (1984). The major weakness with this proposal is that it would be much more difficult to establish whether the mechanisms were being used effectively than whether they had been set up.

Nevertheless, such an approach is being considered in Australia. A working party on PIs recommended to the Australian Vice-Chancellors' Committee (1988) that student evaluations of teaching and curriculum should be developed in two ways: 'Rating by students on a small number of defined aspects of teaching and of subjects, as indicators of the perceived quality and relevance of teaching and the curriculum; the number of formative evaluations (excluding those done for the overall evaluation) per subject taught and per member of staff in a department as an indicator of commitment to teaching' (AVCC/ACDP 1988). Considerable work has been conducted in Australia under the Higher Education Performance Indicators Research Project. Course evaluation questionnaires have been developed that, it is claimed, provide a reliable and valid teaching PI for the higher education system.

In the USA, Kells (1989), Jordan and Ory and Parker all refer to the large amount of data that is being requested now by various bodies, including accrediting bodies and state legislators: 'all colleges and universities are currently facing three demands for information: evaluation, accreditation and assessment' (Ory and Parker, p.385). They quote the suggestion that the various agencies requiring the information should work towards co-operative agreement regarding how records will be kept, how data will be arrayed and how to combine efforts at data collection, analysis and presentation. As similar demands grow in the UK there could be an important role for one set of PIs. The Morris Report stated that, 'a system of performance indicators cannot flourish in the absence of a comprehensive range of statistics, ratios, costs and similar forms of information. For that reason, the Committee recommends the establishment of an integrated Higher Education Statistical Record, covering colleges, polytechnics and universities' (paragraph 6.15).

Summary

In this chapter we have discussed ways of assessing teaching performance through the use of performance indicators. These are likely to be more practicable than the attempts at computing the private or social rate of return to investment in higher education discussed in Chapter 1. We first examined the potential of 'value-added', of which there has been some development and use in the USA and some signs of support in the UK; the need for further research and development in this area has been noted. We analysed the use of cost measures as performance indicators and particularly highlighted the problems of measuring output. We then noted the problems associated with the use of wastage rates, a superficially straightforward PI. So, too, were employment and first destination statistics found to be subject to several criticisms. Finally, we examined student and peer review.

For several PIs reference was made to the work of J. Johnes and Taylor. They conclude (1990) that none of these variables 'is useful as a PI *per se*' because most of the output variation between universities is determined by differences in inputs. The indicators developed in their book are, they suggest, more acceptable measures of performance since they at least take account of inputs and examine the differences between expected and actual outputs. However, they believe, the remaining 'unexplained' variation between universities is relatively small and more rigourous tests would be required before the indicators 'could be regarded as sufficiently robust to be used for resource allocation purposes.'

We conclude that neither singly nor as a group do PIs for teaching emerge as being well developed, but there has been progress in recent years. If PIS are to be applied for research, it is essential that adequate account is taken of teaching performance if an imbalance of priorities is to be avoided.

Chapter 4

Surveys of Performance Indicators of Research

4.1 Assessing Research Performance

The development of PIs of research reflects a complex mixture of technical advances and policy changes, in particular, the place of evaluation of research performance should be viewed against changes in the funding of UK universities in recent years. In 1981, major cuts were announced in funding through the reduction in the recurrent grant. These cuts involved an average 17% reduction over the university system as whole over a three year period, but ranged from 44% to 6% in individual universities.

It was thought after these 1981 cuts that universities would be allowed level funding. This, however, did not materialise and against a background of still further cuts in real terms, the UGC in November 1984 (Circular Letter 17/84) began a review of grant distribution, with particular reference to research. In May 1985 (Circular Letter 12/85: *Planning for the Late 1980s*) universities were asked to detail their future plans. The letter postulated an annual decline of funding in real terms of two per cent per annum. The letter made clear that there was to be evaluation so as to facilitate selective funding, which was necessary to 'maintain the quality' of university research.

Universities were asked to give details of their research plans and priorities, their planning machinery and research profiles of individual subject areas (by cost centre). This last section specifically requested details of: the numbers of research staff and research students; the titles of not more than five recent books or articles, or other comparable examples of research achievement, which the university would regard as typical of the best of its research in the subject area; any explanation or justification of priorities in terms of likely economic or social benefit, advancement of the discipline, or in any other terms; and any other relevant indicators of research performance.

Just before its deadline date of the end of November 1985, the UGC published in Circular Letter 22/85 details of the resource allocation process. This followed much criticism of the secrecy surrounding the UGC's decision-making, including its resource allocation processes.

The circular described a procedure whereby the allocation was made up of elements related to teaching-based criteria (T), research-based criteria (R) and special factors (S). The research-based criteria were identified as: resourcing related to staff and student numbers (SR) - termed the 'floor' provision element; resourcing based on income from Research Councils and charitable bodies (DR); resourcing related to contract research income (CR); and resourcing selectively distributed on judgement (JR). The judgement factor appears to have been based on 'peer reviews', the universities' own submissions, New Blood posts awarded to departments and the advice of external advisers and 'a wide range of other indicators' (letter Chairman of UGC, 1.8.86). The results of this exercise were announced by the UGC in 1986.

In Chapter 2 it was noted firstly that in many countries there was a move towards a more selective funding of research, and secondly, during a period of declining, or even level, funding, an emphasis is placed on the search for more objective decision aids to use when making more selective funding decisions. Referring to the purposes of PIs, SCRI in its consultative document, *Issues in Quantitative Assessment of Departmental Research* (1989) claimed that 'relatively objective data can be used both to assist the forming of judgements and to strengthen their public acceptability.' The claim was also made that the UK was the first to experience these pressures. The Report from the UFC on the 1989 Research Assessment Exercise admits that the 1985/6 exercise 'was probably the first attempt in any country to make a comprehensive assessment of the quality of university research. It is not surprising that it was imperfect and came in for criticism' (p.2).

The pressure to evaluate research was felt across the board in the UK in the 1980s and led to an interest in the technical developments in bibliometrics which might permit policy-relevant use of measurement of publications and citations. At that time, the work of Martin and Irvine in analysing the convergence of partial indicators for comparing similar 'big science' facilities attracted wide attention in the UK (Phillips and Turney 1988, p.192). As a result of these factors, the ABRC and the Economic and Social Research Council, commissioned a series of studies of bibliometric techniques. Each is described in detail in a special edition of the journal *Scientometrics* devoted to developments in the UK (Volume 14, No. 3-4 1988). The third study produced bibliometric profiles of all publicly financed civil laboratories in the UK including those in universities and polytechnics. The researchers claimed 'the underlying objective was to test whether reliable research output indicators could be produced which might help the Research Councils and other funding agencies in determining future policies' (Carpenter et al 1988, p.217).

These technical developments were obviously of interest to the various groups responsible for conducting selectivity exercises. At the Science Policy Support Group (SPSG) seminar held at the end of 1987 to discuss university research PIs and the 1985/6 UGC exercise it was pointed out that 'a great deal of published work on research evaluation already exists and that many of the issues raised during the seminar have already been the subject of sophisticated discourse. It is important that the UGC/UFC should be more fully informed of these sources before the next evaluation exercise' (Smyth and Anderson 1987, p.21).

Some of the research councils took considerable interest in developing bibliometric indicators with National Environmental Research Council (NERC) and Agricultural and Food Research Council (AFRC) leading the field (Anderson 1989). There are various overlaps between the pressures on higher education and on the Research Councils to develop PIs (Cave and Hanney 1990) and PIs will be used by Research Councils when they evaluate the research centres they support within higher education institutions.

The role of indicators has been less important in subject reviews than in the selectivity exercises. Nevertheless, there was still a role for them and although in the Oxburgh Review the earth scientists were asked to undertake citation analysis of their own work, the UGC felt it was important to validate and further analyse the material. The bibliometric study by the Science and Engineering Policy Studies Unit (SEPSU) on the whole supported the decisions which had been made and, according to Anderson, the unpublished report drew some useful methodological conclusions for future bibliometric exercises. These included the need for comprehensive publications lists to be obtained directly from university departments because at least half the output of earth sciences departments was missed by the *Science Citation Index* (SCI).

The coming together of technical advances and policy requirements for the development of research PIs was especially strong in the creation by the CVCP/UGC PIs Steering Committee of the Sub-Committee on Research Indicators (SCRI). In composition it combined those who had been responsible for developing PIs on behalf of the CVCP/UGC with experts on bibliometrics including John Irvine from the Science Policy Research Unit (SPRU) at Sussex University. This is a good illustration of the development in the late 1980s of a network of groups with overlapping membership which are examining the potential role of various research PIs. SCRI has a number of tasks including: encouraging each university to set up an appropriate publications database which could be called upon when necessary; exploring which data on research output might be included in the annual volume of management statistics and PIs; and studying ways in which bibliometric methods might be used to assist judgements about the quality of research.

The UGC/UFC prepared much more thoroughly for the 1989 research selectivity exercise. A comprehensive review of the criticisms of the 1986 exercise was undertaken and included in a consultative document (UGC Circular Letter, 15/88). Nearly 300 responses were received and taken into account in the Circular Letter (UGC, 45/88) requesting details on: staff; publications and other public outputs; students and studentships; research grants and contracts; a statement of research plans and general observations. Explicit guidelines were issued on how to compile these data and, in the case of staff, students and research income, detailed questionnaires were sent. The letter stated that:

> 'The main criteria to be used in determining ratings are:
>
> (i) publications and other publicly identifiable output;
>
> (ii) success in obtaining research grants and studentships;
>
> (iii) success in obtaining research contracts;
>
> (iv) professional knowledge and judgement of advisory group and panel members, supplemented where appropriate by advice from outside experts.
>
> The general approach will therefore be that of an informed peer review'.

The ratings were given on a five point scale (5 - 1) with a common standard of interpretation across all units of assessments. The purpose of the selectivity exercise was to produce new JR values to influence the distribution of the research element of UFC funding from 1990/91. The proportion of research funding to be allocated selectively is being raised by increasing the ratio of JR to SR from approximately 1:1 to 2:1.

Thus we have witnessed a gradual, if controversial, introduction of the use of performance indicators (with particular emphasis on research indicators) into judgements which influence the UGC's resource allocation process. This chapter discusses in more detail the major research performance indicators, some of which were used by the UGC/UFC.

It is also worth noting that the second (1987) statement of the joint CVCP/UGC Working Group on performance indicators identified only two 'research based' indicators for inclusion in the 1987 list and these were still the only two in the 1990 publication. The first of these - research income - is discussed in section 4.4 below. The second is 'research postgraduates as a percentage of full-time equivalent students'. This indicator is a measure of the attractiveness of a department or institution to potential research students. Numbers will however depend on availability of grants (and thus on research council policy), and there will be wide variations across disciplines. The indicator is also linked, as a measure of inputs, with completion rates of research degrees, discussed in Chapter 3.5 above. In the 1989 research selectivity exercise numbers of research students and of successful doctoral thesis submissions were according to the UFC Report, 'thought by many panels to be significant indicators of research quality' (paragraph 25).

Very little attention was given to PIs of research in the PCFC Reports on Research and on PIs. Its Research Committee of Enquiry (Roith 1990) did suggest however that 'the distribution of any additional resources allocated by Council should be carried out following advice from an Advisory Group on Research to the Chief Executive. In determining allocations the group might pay attention to such parameters as: recent income from industry, commerce, the public sector; the level of support received from research councils; the number of postgraduate research students. In using such parameters, however, it is important that quality is considered and the Advisory Group will have a key role to play here.'

Before considering specific research PIs it is important to note some of the various debates that surround the notion of 'research performance'. Phillimore (1989) proposes four aspects of 'performance' and matches the relevant indicators to them: output (publications); impact (citations); quality (research council grants; research studentships; awards, prizes, honours, etc.; committee memberships; journal editorships; peer judgement; reputation); utility (external income; parents, licenses; contract/external staff). Although some of these points are taken into account in the discussion of specific indicators, there is possibly more agreement about the validity of most research PIs than there is about those for teaching. There is some unease in the social sciences and arts and humanities that a system of indicators designed to show research performance in the natural sciences, is being inappropriately applied to them (see, for example, Minogue 1986). There is some overlap between this argument and that advanced by Elton (1988a) that scholarship forms a third strand in the activities of universities, and is a vital link between teaching and research. Scholarship, the new interpretation of what is already known, is least prevalent in applied sciences and most common in the humanities. The idea that scholarship should be treated separately was considered but explicitly rejected in the Kingman Report.

4.2 Output Measures: Publications, Licenses and Patents

The publications of a department have always been an important informal indication of research activity. This is shown in, for example, the lists of publications which figure in many universities' annual reports in both the UK and the USA. The indicator of research output has been formulated in many ways, some of which represent attempts to improve its usefulness and overcome the perceived disadvantages of previous formulations.

In order to calculate the indicator, decisions have to be made concerning: the types of publication to be included; the weightings to be given to the various types of publication; sources of information about the publications; and whether to count the total publications for the department or for each academic member of staff. The 1986 statement of the CVCP/UGC Working Group also suggested that the percentage of staff in a cost centre who had not published during the preceding three years could be a PI.

These technical issues become particularly controversial when the performance indicators form a potential element in resource allocation or when they affect public reputations, rather than remain a purely academic exercise. As an illustration of the consequences of their use, one study of British university publication rates was not published in the journal for which it was originally accepted for fear of possible litigation (Crewe 1987).

There are two broad approaches to the types of publication to include. Either a range of publications is examined or the study is limited to journals. If a range of publications is used then it could include: books, journal articles, conference papers and, exceptionally, reviews (Cartter 1966). Even when a range of publications is used, it is difficult to include contributions to edited books although some studies (for example, Gillett 1986; UFC 1989 Research Selectivity Exercise) have done so. Crewe (1987) revised his paper to include contributions to books edited by British political scientists but found that it made little difference to his original rankings.

Usually a scoring mechanism has to be devised to weight the various types of contributions (see for example, Crewe 1987; Glenn and Villemez 1970; Harris, G. 1989; Knudsen and Vaughan 1969; Rasmussen 1985). Some of these can be fairly sophisticated; for example, Glenn and Villemez weighted the score given to a sociology department for its published books (if they were reviewed in the *American Sociological Review*) according to the average quality of the journal articles of the department. This was measured by asking sociologists to assess the importance of various journals in which the department's articles appeared and scoring the departments accordingly. The CVCP/UGC Working Group originally suggested that 'publications should be categorised by type, for example, book, contribution in major/minor journal, broadcast talk, etc'. This approach has been continued in the two trial exercises conducted by SCRI. In autumn 1988, all university departments of chemistry, economics, history and physics were asked to provide comprehensive lists of their published output for the calendar year 1987. Universities were given 11 headings under which to put the number of publications of the department: papers in academic journals; letters in academic journals; articles in professional journals; articles in popular journals; books; edited books; published official reports; contributions to edited works; contributions to conference proceedings; other publications; contributions in other media. SCRI has not attempted to develop a scoring to weight such a variety of contributions and is not expected to do so when the full database is produced. Johnes (1988) argued that the validity of weighting systems would be increased if compilers reported the findings using various weighting schemes. This approach was adopted by Crewe.

Different subjects seem to favour different forms of publication, and these preferences are related to the varying nature of subjects - as discussed in Biglan's (1973) typology. Many assessments of publications, especially in science and engineering and in some social sciences, are compiled from journal articles alone: for example, Frame (1983) for sciences and mechanical engineering; Jones et al (1982) for biological sciences; Drew and Karpf (1981) for physics, history, mathematics and chemistry; Laband (1985), Johnes (1986a), Liebowitz and Palmer (1984) and Bell and Seater (1978) for economics; Cox and Catt (1977) for psychology; Rogers and Scratcherd (1986) for anatomy and physiology.

The analysis of journals can involve a variety of techniques irrespective of whether a range of publications or journals alone are considered. Crewe included all the journals in which British political scientists had published, which amounted to almost 200, whereas Knudsen and

Vaughan used three leading journals and Cox and Catt used only the 13 published by the American Psychological Association. Glenn and Villemez included journals on the basis of their questionnaire described above. Drew and Karpf, and Liebowitz and Palmer included those journals with the highest average number of citations per article ie those with the greatest impact. Some studies, for example, Frame, included all the journal articles appearing in various indexes.

It is thus clear that many authors use an implicit quality weighting system (one for recognised journals, zero for omitted ones). Some take quality adjustment further. Glenn and Villemez used six different scores for the various journals included. Others, for example, Drew and Karpf or Johnes (1986a), made no distinction among the leading journals (20 in each case) that they included.

Some studies consider the number of pages (using a formula to take account of differing page sizes and, sometimes, differing average length of articles in the various journals) in addition to the number of articles produced. Bell and Seater suggested, however, that, 'it seems that the article and page methods are virtually identical'. Crewe also found little difference between the rank ordering based on the aggregate page length of all publications and that based on the number of publications.

The types of publications used influence (and, as Bell and Seater show, can be influenced by) the source of information about the number of publications to be included. Various methods are used to calculate productivity: abstracts, indexes, self-reporting, examination of the journals, books reviewed in leading journals, etc.

Most studies give greater attention to the score for each member of the department than to the departmental total, but some (for example, Jones in a major American multidisciplinary study and Rogers and Scratcherd) count only the latter. Publications with more than one author can have their score divided, as for example by Laband and Crewe, or, if the authors are in different institutions, each institution can gain the full score (see, for example, Glenn and Villemez). In the SCRI trial exercise attempts have been made to take account of the distortions introduced by multiple authorship of publications: universities have been asked to count both on a whole and a fractional basis. The latter is regarded as the most appropriate form of analysis but is time consuming and difficult logistically because of the volume of data. It is unlikely, therefore, 'that publications will be fractionated when the full publications database is established' (Anderson, p.105). Most studies credit the department of which the author was a member when the publication appeared but some, for example, Bell and Seater, or Laband credit the Department at which the author is currently based. However, when Bell and Seater compared their approach with that of Niemi (1975), who researched at much the same time with a similar coverage, but attributing articles to the department at which the author was based at the time of publication, they found the results were similar. In its 1989 research selectivity exercise the UFC was keen to check on any changes in staff compared with those for whom the production figures related. In its report on the exercise it recognised that attributing all the output to the department at which the author was based at the 'census date would have the added benefit of giving due weight to departmental endeavours to improve the level and quality of research activity' (paragraph 40).

In some areas it is vital to count the number of patents, licence agreements and copyrights in the same way as publications. But this often creates serious problems of data collection, and the problem of weighting patents, for example, is even more difficult than that of weighting publications.

The period over which publications are counted also varies greatly, ranging from 13 years in Laband to only one year in the study by Gillett. For the 1989 exercise the preceding five years were considered.

According to Gillett (1986), with reference to the UK, publications provide 'the most valid, fair and direct way to compare the research performance of departments'. In a 1989 study of various PIs Gillett concluded that only those based on journal peer review, ie articles in journals, constitute PIs that are capable of yielding a reasonably valid measure of departmental performance. Yet the measurement of publications has only begun fairly recently. The ranking of doctoral programmes by the American Council on Education (ACE) carried out by Cartter (1966) and Roose and Andersen (1970) were primarily reputational rankings (although Cartter provided publication assessments in a few subjects). These rankings led to many attempts to develop objective rankings of departments based on publications and to compare with and improve on the subjective reputational rankings. Cox and Catt found that 'subjective measurements based upon 'reputation' and 'opinion' are intuitively unsatisfying, and our study showed that there can be large and dramatic differences in ratings based on objective measurement of productivity'.

Publication of the 1986 UGC research rankings also encouraged the preparation of research output measures, which were set alongside the UGC rankings. These exercises indicated considerable divergences particularly in the humanities and social sciences - see for example, Sheppard et al for German, or Gillett for psychology. Crewe also concluded that the correlation between the UGC rankings and departmental publications rates was 'at most, patchy'. Harris, M. (1986) noted that the UGC rankings have proved to be more acceptable in the sciences and engineering but, even here, Rogers and Scratcherd produced objective rankings based on publications in anatomy and physiology that differ strongly from the UGC rankings. Frame, too, in America, suggested that quantitative evaluations, especially those based on publications and citations, had advantages over reputational rankings in science and engineering. The various exercises at producing research output measures in the UK in 1986 were described and discussed at the SPSG seminar on the 1986 research selectivity exercise (Smyth and Anderson) and were analysed by Phillimore (1989). He listed the characteristics of each study, which displayed considerable variations in the criteria used.

The UGC rankings were not entirely reputational but were also based on an assessment of five publications for each cost centre and many other factors including the support from research councils, foundations, government departments and other bodies, and a range of indicators such as New Blood posts and published tables in academic journals. Insofar as emphasis was placed on the five representative research publications, it has been strongly argued that the use of such a technique is faulty, and that total publications provide a better PI of research. According to Phillimore, this was common ground amongst all the critics. Sheppard et al clearly show that German departments in Schools of Modern Languages in new universities suffered from being part of a larger submission, compared with separate departments in more traditional universities where the German departments were allowed to provide five publications for German alone. Similarly, Gillett shows how the system of providing five publications favoured larger departments and that the UGC attempted to hide this. In rebuttal of this proposition Sizer told the meeting organised by the SPSG that the demand for a list of five works was mainly intended to identify weaker centres, some of which could not even muster this many publications for scrutiny (*Times Higher Education Supplement*, 4 December 1987). Rankings based on total departmental publication output rather than per capita output are at least open about the impact of size. Rogers and Scratcherd, for example, have argued that:

> 'The measurement of research activity by output is direct, open and fair. By introducing a heavy reliance on conspicuous expenditure and on personal judgements of the worth of particular types of research, the UGC has substituted a complicated, hidden process.'

The attention paid by the UGC to these various criticisms has been noted. A more sophisticated approach was adopted in asking for information about publications in Circular Letter 45/88. Each relevant staff member was invited to nominate up to two books, book chapters or journal articles and publications considered to be of major significance in the field could be marked with an asterisk. Each department was also asked to submit totals for each of the three publications categories. Staff were also requested to list, if appropriate, not more than two other forms of public output. Possible examples of such output were given: computer software/languages; conference proceedings; engineering designs; musical compositions; paintings/sculptures; patents; copyrights; licence agreements; translations of published work from other languages.

In the count of total departmental publications in the three main categories no attempt was made to fractionate the publication counts according to the number of co-authors. Precautions were taken to ensure that publications were not 'double counted' (eg where staff in the same department were co-authors) and publication counts were expressed per staff member.

Crewe and many of the American studies suggest that there is often quite a high correlation between rankings based on total departmental publications and reputational rankings (for example, Cartter, Jones) but not such a good correlation when the publications per capita are considered. This suggests that the *per capita* method has an advantage in presenting a picture that is not distorted by size and it is the approach being adopted by SCRI.

As a PI of research, publications can provide useful information to policy makers. Frame argued that quantitative indicators could enable managers to make fine-tuned adjustments to research and development efforts. Crewe suggested that by discounting the most productive 20% of a department's staff, a measure could be obtained of the collective strength of a department and that departments with the strongest collective strength should be given priority by the UGC, since individually strong members of other departments could be supported by individual grants. Johnes (1986a) claimed that the value of publications as a PI is that 'it points to those factors which enhance research productivity'. These factors, which will be of interest to policy makers, include optimal staffing levels, library stocks and staff-student ratios. Hare and Wyatt (1988) claim that the factors determining departmental research output are still not well known and it could be dangerous to pursue major restructuring policies without such knowledge. PIs could, as Johnes has shown, be useful in identifying such factors.

Recently SEPSU produced the first detailed analysis of how university departments spend money on research. The author of the report, Peter Collins, insisted, according to the *Times Higher Education Supplement* (12 October 1990) that the findings, 'nail forever the idea of economies of scale in research - the notion, which has driven a succession of policies for rationalising science departments, that the large departments are more productive than small ones.' Although there is a threshold below which a department cannot be viable, being in a bigger department does nothing to provide researchers with more support staff, capital spending or other inputs which size is meant to ensure. Furthermore, several recent projects at SPRU used bibliometric methods to examine some of the factors influencing research productivity that are relevant to the current policy of concentrating resources. Hicks and Skea (1989) for example investigated the research productivity of departments of physics in the wake of the restructuring of earth science departments and the Edwards Report (1988) *The Future of University Physics*. They concluded that: 'on the one hand there appears to be evidence that, overall, larger departments are more productive, on the other hand, this dependence is extremely weak and can easily be explained by departmental characteristics not related to size.' However, evidence from Johnes and Taylor (1990a) suggests that a statistical analysis of the results of the 1989 research selectivity exercise demonstrates that economies of scale exist in research. This finding is examined, and questioned, in Chapter 4.5.

In Australia the policy of concentrating research resources in economics in research centres was examined by Harris, G., (1989). His study of research output revealed that, once allowance was made for the greater research time available in research centres, they were not any more productive.

The inclusion of patents, licences and copyrights is particularly important as a way of ensuring that adequate recognition is given to departments whose work is largely orientated towards practical rather than theoretical work. Blume and Sinclair (1973) showed that those engaged on theoretical work were more likely to gain recognition.

Some of the results of rankings based on publications have been so unexpected (for example, Robey's (1979) study of American politics departments) that they have undermined the credibility of publications as a measure of activity. It is argued that even though some publication rankings take some account of quality (for example, by counting articles only in top journals; by using different weightings; by counting books reviewed only in top journals; or by using the citations impact of journals) they are not a real measure of the quality of research carried out by a department. There is also a danger that a concentration on the number of publications produced will lead to an over-production of poor quality articles. Such a fact was highlighted by Collini (1989) in the article *Publish and Be Dimmed.* More fundamental questions are often raised about the extent to which publications are a valid reflection of scientific achievement (see, for example, Gibbons and Georghiou 1987; Phillips 1989).

Furthermore, there are many technical problems involved in devising a satisfactory method of assessing publications. A wide range of publications creates problems of scoring the various types of publications and implies that all journal articles are of equal worth. Including only a narrow range of 'top' journals may mean that books are ignored and that those who concentrate in specific fields are penalised. Seminal articles will not be given due weight. There is also the problem of favouritism in journal publishing practices, although Crewe could find very little evidence of this. If the generally more satisfactory approach of counting publications *per capita* is to be used it raises the difficulty of who exactly should be classed as a member of the department. What, for example, is the position of research staff? Various authors (see, for example, Ziman 1989; Hare and Wyatt 1988) question the appropriateness of per capita figures when, according to Lotka's law a high proportion of output comes from a small number of researchers. Crewe showed however that this did not have a major impact on the ranking of government departments, and, anyway, could be discounted if necessary.

The importance of the weighting issue is demonstrated in the study by Johnes, G., (1990) of research output in UK Departments of Economics over the period 1984-1988. This study was commissioned by the Royal Economic Society and prepared in connection with the UFC's 1989 evaluation of research. Johnes identified four different measures of staff input and 30 measures of departmental research output, based upon alternative weighting schemes. This yielded a total of 120 measures of *per capita* research output. Examination of the rankings produced by each measure showed that the 40 departments concerned can be broken down into a group of 14 whose ranking was fairly insensitive to the weighting system used, and a larger group of 26 where the ranking fluctuated violently. For example, the Department of Economics at Brunel was ranked fourth in the weighting scheme most favourable to it and 39th in the least favourable. The study illustrates the importance of choice of weights and the potential dangers of manipulation of them.

As the CVCP/UGC Working Group recognised, a particular problem arises in the case of patents or licence agreements in those institutions where commercial 'arms', in the sense of limited companies, have been set up to handle the products of the department. The limited company is legally an entirely separate entity, yet insofar as the base for its existence may be the success of the work undertaken in the department, it would not seem reasonable to regard its products as other than 'belonging' to the department. Where individual companies relating to individual departments have been set up (possibly under the umbrella of a holding company) it may be relatively easy to establish where particular products belong; however, where individuals from different departments were the prime movers in eventual commercial success this may not be easy.

With a few exceptions - for example, Rasmussen - publications rankings have not been used much in providing intra-institutional comparisons. As many have shown (see Frame; Drew and Karpf, and Smith and Fiedler 1971) different subjects have different publication rates. This suggests the need for a concerted, system-wide approach to defining and calculating the performance indicator. Furthermore, publication practices vary widely between different fields of the same subject.

Our discussion has left open the important practical question of the cost of preparation of comparative data. However it is clear that most institutions presently collect data on publications for their own records. There is therefore no reason why it could not be processed according to agreed procedures and collected centrally, although detailed instructions are needed to ensure consistency and this is what SCRI is attempting to establish. This method has the disadvantage of involving self-reporting. An alternative approach is to use abstracting or equivalent services, though the cost of doing so would be greater.

In certain subjects, including political science (*Times Higher Education Supplement*, 10 November 1989), there is unease about the accuracy of the publications figures produced in the 1989 selectivity exercise using the self-reporting method. The UFC report stated 'it has become apparent that the assumptions of honesty and veracity was not always justified and in one or two subject areas, at least, it would seem that deliberate 'misreporting' occurred' (paragraph 24). The misreporting included:

(i) altering the date of publication to bring a book or article within the review period;

(ii) claiming authorship of edited books;

(iii) claiming sole authorship of co-authored publications;

(iv) inclusion of publications representing research undertaken in another institution.

The report suggests that in any future exercise there would have to be arrangements within universities for enhancing the likelihood of accuracy and enabling subsequent checking by the UFC. It argues that the creation of a standard publications database in universities well ahead of the next exercise would reduce the risk of error. As we have noted, this is what SCRI is working towards.

4.3 Measuring Quality/Impact

We discussed earlier in this chapter the problems associated with using an index of the number of publications which a department produces as a measure of research performance. Perhaps the most important objection to the use of a quantity index is that the number of articles published is only a measure of quantity and, as a result, the relative quality of articles is ignored. What is required therefore is a means of adjusting the number of articles published for their relative quality.

One such method of quality adjustment is to count the number of citations which are obtained by a department or individual over a given time period. It has been argued by many authors that citations provide an objective way of assessing the relative quality or, more precisely, the impact or influence of research output (see, for example, Laband 1985 and Moed et al 1985).

The economic basis of using a citation as an indicator of quality lies in the analogy with market signalling behaviour (Laband 1985). During the process of research, relevant literature is surveyed and articles selected for citation on the basis of their relative 'quality'. Quality may be taken as the degree to which the cited articles have made an impact on and improved understanding in the subject area. In this sense, the researcher has revealed a preference for the work cited and this may be taken as an indicator of its quality relative to other publications in the subject area. This procedure entails a presumption that quality depends on the extent to which research is used. As we shall see later such an interpretation has been criticised and Cozzens (1989, p.437) recently asked whether citations 'measure quality, importance, impact, influence, utility, visibility, all of the above, or something else?'

A number of studies have been carried out to establish empirical evidence on the relationship between citation counts and various measures of quality.

Sher and Garfield (1966) looked at the work of Nobel Prize winners in physics, chemistry and medicine between 1962 and 1963. Counting citations for 1961 (to exclude the effect of attaining the Nobel Prize on the citation rate) they found that the 30 Nobel Prize winners were cited 30 times more frequently than the average for their fields. On average there were 5.51 citations an author (excluding Nobel Prize winners) whereas the Nobel Prize winners secured an average of 169 citations. Even discounting the frequency of publication, since the Nobel Prize winners published more often, they found that the Nobel Prize winners had an average of 2.9 citations per article whereas the average rate for the subject area was 1.57.

Garfield (1977) later extended this study to include Nobel Prize winners for the period 1961 to 1975, covering all sciences. Again, taking the citation rates for 1961, the average citation rate for the prize winners was 2877 whereas taking an average for other authors over the period 1970 to 1974 led them to expect a citation rate of something less than 50.

As a corollary to these studies Garfield also attempted to determine whether scientists who are highly cited are more likely to be honoured by their peers. Using a list of the 50 most cited authors (later extended to 250 most cited authors), Garfield (1970) found that 17% turned out to be Nobel Prize winners and 60% were elected to at least one national academy of science. Of the sample considered, 38% won neither of these awards.

Indirect evidence of the relationship between quality and citation indices is provided by Bayer and Folger (1966) using a sample of biochemistry doctorates (granted in 1957 and 1958). The citation counts of those awarded doctorates were correlated with peer judgements as to the quality of the awarding institution taken from a previous study. The results suggested a positive and highly significant correlation between the citations received by those holding the doctorates and the quality of the awarding institution.

Further evidence is supplied by Clark (1954) who asked a panel of experts in psychology to list the people who in their opinion had made the most significant impact on their field. The index which the experts supplied was then correlated with judgements indexed by various measures including citation rates, papers published, income and quality of students. It was found that the citation rate had a positive correlation with the index provided by the experts, and also that the citation index had a stronger correlation with the index provided by the experts than any of the other measures.

This evidence led Garfield to conclude that of all the variables that can influence citation rates, the scientific quality of the work published is the dominant one (1979). More recently Narin (1987), another leading proponent of citations analysis claimed that 'the results of bibliometric studies are seldom counter-intuitive: they usually agree with expert expectations.' Such agreement, however, might still leave room for differing interpretations of the meanings of citations. Nederhof and Van Raan (1989) review the points made by critics such as MacRoberts and MacRoberts (1986) that citations are often either rhetoric instruments 'used not to convince others by the strength of arguments but to persuade them by non-logical means' or they are 'ceremonial citations' which are 'references made to individuals whose work has not actually been influential, but to whom the citer feels obliged' (p.427). A comparison was made between bibliometric indicators of productivity and impact and the results of peer review process - the awarding of a cum laude degree to graduates in chemistry. Highly significant differences in impact and productivity were obtained between the cum laudes and the non-cum laudes. It is unlikely there would be differential ceremonial or persuasive value in a citation towards the work of a graduate student. Therefore Nederhof and Van Raan conclude 'even though a percentage of the citations may have been given for perfunctory or negative reasons, these results support the contention that when sufficiently large numbers of papers are examined, citations counts may provide a useful partial indicator of quality, and can be used fruitfully to monitor scientific research' (p.435).

Citations data are collected by the Institute for Scientific Information (ISI) and published annually in the Science Citations Index (SCI). Data are collected on citations of books and articles from over 5,200 journals and information is provided on citation counts which include, for each author, the number and source of each citation and, for each journal, the number of times the journal is cited and the average number of citations an article published in a particular journal will receive (the journal's impact factor). This data base has been the source of information for most of the citation studies carried out, and would almost certainly be that used for any concurrent calculation of citation rates for the purposes of evaluating research performance.

The use of citations analysis at Leiden University was referred to in Chapter 2.2. It is described in some detail here to illustrate various points. Moed et al (1985) used the SCI to compile citations data for the faculties of Medicine and Mathematics/Natural Sciences of the University of Leiden in Holland for the period 1970 to 1980. The data handled included 5,700 publications and 42,000 citations. The procedure used to count citations was in essence to compile a list of publications and search the SCI for citations.

Moed et al. encountered several problems in compiling the data. First, they found that missing data accounted for about 10% of the sample, but that, more importantly, these omissions affected several individual departments more seriously than others. An example provided by Moed et al. was that a programming error had resulted in all citations to a number of journals being omitted. These accounted for only 3% of the total sample, yet for the departments which published in these journals up to 50% of the citations were omitted because of this error. This problem is exacerbated when a highly cited article is missed from the publications list.

The second problem encountered by Moed et al. was that the research units studied were often small, of the order of two to 10 researchers. As a result, relatively few publications were produced and, as a consequence, only a small number of citations recorded. In these circumstances, small errors or omissions can lead to misleading conclusions. Moed et al. argued that this problem can be overcome to a large extent by aggregating research groups, but at a high cost of loss of information.

Moed et al. finally obtained 99% completeness of citations of articles published from Leiden, and maintain that in order properly to evaluate small university research groups this level of completeness is required. However, much effort was expended to achieve this degree of accuracy; if citation indexes are to be calculated as a matter of course in order to evaluate research performance, they would prove expensive. This is an important consideration when evaluating the usefulness of a PI for the purpose of resource allocation or simply for continuous assessment. Citation studies may however, play a role in major reviews of particular subject areas and in the development of strategies for subject area rationalisation.

The problem of how to allocate citations has been highlighted by Laband (1985). It has been the practice when constructing citation counts to examine the articles published from a source, as in the Leiden study quoted above. Laband maintains that this may not be a good indicator of how well a department is likely to perform in the future, since some of the members of the department who published in previous years may no longer be there, and may have been replaced by new researchers with altogether different levels of research output. He therefore argues that in order to evaluate a department's future performance we need to allocate the citations record of the current members of that department. Future research performance will be related to the present composition of research staff, not to an average over some previous time period.

A further practical difficulty is to choose the journals from which to record citations. As Johnes (1986a), points out, in relation to a quantity index, 'too few might bias the results in favour of departments which produce research which is of general interest at the expense of departments which produce specialised research of equally high quality. On the other hand, the inclusion of too many would imply that an article in a relatively obscure journal is in some sense worth as much as the most prestigious serials.' In principle this problem also applies to citations. How many journals should be surveyed and what is the appropriate weight that should be applied to citations from journals of varying quality?

Numerous schemes for weighting quantity of output have been applied in the literature. One example related to citation indexing is provided by Jones et al (1982) in their assessment of biology research doctorate programmes in the United States, and the method proposed also provides a convenient and computationally less difficult method of calculating citation indices. It has been noted that the SCI provides data on the 'impact factor' of each journal. The impact factor is based on the average number of citations which an article in a particular journal is likely to receive. For each journal the average influence per paper is calculated by working out the average number of times papers in the journal are cited, each citation having first been weighed by the influence weight of the citing journal, ie a citation from an influential journal is scored more highly than one from an obscure journal. The influence weight of a journal is in turn defined as 'the weighted number of citations it receives from other journals, normalised by the numbers of references it gives' (Carpenter et al 1988, p.216). High profile journals are likely to have higher impact factors and this can be taken as an indication that articles selected for publication in these journals are of a higher quality.

A citations index can be calculated by multiplying the number of articles published in a particular journal by the associated impact factor. This procedure is computationally much easier than compiling citation indexes by author, since it requires only the number of articles published in each journal. Thus impact factors provide a very convenient method of adjusting research outputs for quality and it may be argued that impact factors are a more objective measure of a journal's quality than the various subjective methods of assessment which have been applied. Anderson found, however, that the complexity of the journal influence weights system often lost the meaning of the citations to many researchers and sometimes produced suspicious results. Phillips and Turney reported that in relation to the study by Carpenter et al, 'the lack of transparency of the method has made getting to grips with the results take longer than expected, thus partially negating the time advantage of by-passing citations' (p.196).

There has been a very considerable and highly technical debate about the use and value of citations analysis. Many of the issues debated are included in Cozzens' list of factors that might inflate or reduce citations. They include: the effects of timing; journal of publication; self-citation; negative citations; whole, fractional or first name counting; in-group citations; language of publication; obliteration by incorporation; field differences and cross disciplinary citation patterns. Only some of the major points will be considered below using evidence drawn from, amongst others, Aaronson (1975) and Garfield.

In the SCI, citations are listed by senior or primary authors. The citations of junior authors can be counted, but this requires knowledge of the senior author and a search for citations under the senior author's name. Counting junior citations is again likely to be a time-consuming operation. Further, there is the question of the weighting which should be applied to citations of junior authors.

There are number of reasons why a citations count is 'measured with error'. The presumption underlying citations as an indicator of research performance is that a citation indicates a positive quality in the article cited. This need not always be the case. Some citations are negative or derogatory. In an article somewhat modifying his earlier enthusiasm for citations as a robust measure of quality, Lindsey (1989) referred to the fact that Jensen's controversial paper on racial superiority was one of the most highly cited social science papers. Many of the citations, however, were critical of, or outraged by, the paper primarily because of its political and ethical characteristics. Some citations may be 'sloppy' in the sense that the citing author may not have carried out an exhaustive literature search, or may simply have misunderstood the arguments in the cited article.

One particular potential source of measurement error is self-citation. The analogy made above between citations and market signalling behaviour essentially describes a process of peer review. A citation by a peer indicates recognition of quality. Can self-citations be regarded in this light? In general one might say that self-citations should not be included since they do not, in principle, follow the process of peer review. However, the exclusion of self-citations may introduce a potentially serious bias into the construction of an index for scientists who are researching new or innovative areas, since there may be little or no work, other than their own, to be cited. As Porter (1977) points out, 'self-citations could be used to note the most relevant earlier work, or work with which one is most familiar; they could then reflect real influences or contributions.' Incorrect citations are sometimes given by authors and there can be programming errors made in the SCI. For example in the 1988 Social Science Citation Index the first author of the first edition of this book is incorrectly cited as Cave, S., although the author of the book review in which the citation appears gave the correct name.

Some of these possible sources of error could be eradicated by careful analysis of the data, but, again, the cost of removing even those sources of error which can be identified is likely to be high. However, if these sources of error are not removed, then any index of citations must be treated as random to some degree.

Many writers have argued that citation indices can be used providing there is no systematic bias involved in the measurement of the index. Garfield (1979) argues that 'sloppy, biassed bibliographic practice is a random variable that tends to get cancelled out.' There are other biassing influences but, in general, these measurement errors do not affect one department more than another and as a result a high citation score indicates high quality.

However, whilst it is correct to say that if such influences are random (and more citations indicate higher quality) then citations scores are unbiased, the point estimate obtained for the citation score tells us little about the possible range of values which the citation score may take allowing for the stochastic nature of the variable. In principle, therefore, in order to be able to imply anything about quality of research on the basis of citations scores we need to know the variance associated with citation indices. We could then say with some degree of confidence that a score from a particular department is statistically different from a score obtained from a different department.

Many writers argue that seminal or primordial research may not receive the number of citations which the quality of the research would imply that it should (see Johnes 1986a, MacRoberts and MacRoberts 1986 or Cole and Cole 1972). There are two reasons why this may be the case.

First, it is argued that when an idea becomes accepted universally it requires no formal citation. An example provided by Johnes is that of the concept of Rational Expectations in economics, first proposed by Muth (1961). When referring to Rational Expectations few writers refer to Muth; they are more likely to refer to later applications of Muth's original idea. This is an example of obliteration by incorporation.

Second, the primordial paper may be difficult to understand, since by definition the research is not known to anybody. Subsequent papers which refine the concept may be quoted more freely. In particular, in the area of natural sciences, the primordial paper may be the discovery of a chemical reaction. Subsequent papers may provide easier methods of carrying out an experiment to demonstrate the reaction and as such may be more likely to be cited.

Cole and Cole (1972) argue that the same may be true for radical work which is again by definition contrary to the main trend of thought in any subject area. As a result radical work may not be quoted often or, alternatively, may receive negative citations.

There are two issues related to the weighting of citations: firstly, the relative contributions of co-authors and, secondly, the relative weighting of citations from different articles. These points have been mentioned above and therefore only brief comments will be made here.

In case of co-authorship the issue is what weighting should be applied to each author. Should they have equal weighting, implying that both authors contributed equally to the work? Or should the work of one author be weighted more heavily and, if so, on what basis? Additionally what weight should be applied to a co-authored citation relative to a single authored citation? With respect to journal quality, what weighting do we apply to citations in different journals?

The answers to these questions depend upon the purpose for which the citation index is being derived, and the suitability of any particular weighting scheme must be judged on the basis of prevailing circumstances. What seems certain is that at present we do not have enough information to weight citations in an objective way, and as a result interpretation of citation counts must be done carefully. The possibility of serious error may be reduced by calculating indices based on various weighting schemes to see how sensitive the outcomes are to changes in the weights.

Thus a number of important theoretical and practical difficulties do still exist, and as overcoming these is likely to prove costly and time-consuming, the economic viability of citations indices for concurrent evaluation becomes suspect.

It is also obvious that any bibliometric research involves considerable cost. Work by SPRU at Sussex University contains an indication of what is involved (Martin et al 1985). The SPRU team was requested by the Advisory Board for the Research Councils to conduct detailed bibliometric case studies of two fairly small scientific fields - ocean currents and protein crystallography. The studies involved a survey of publications and citations in the relevant fields over a period of years, using the 'manual' method of inspecting selected journals. The results showed how the quantity and 'quality' of UK research output had fared over time, compared with those of other countries. It was also possible to compare institutions within the UK, although in such small fields there are comparatively few research centres. The SPRU team estimate that the cost of such a study for special fields involving 50 to 100 UK researchers is of the order of £3000-£4000. Laband's major study of 50 US economics departments, which involved collection of citation data for each faculty member, absorbed the time of two individuals on a virtually full-time basis for three months. Data collection and preparation for Crewe's study of British political science departments, which did not involve citation data, was comparatively inexpensive - costing less than £2,000. It would be simple to adjust Crewe's study by using journal 'impact factors' as quality weights. This suggests that the 'impact factor' approach may be an inexpensive short cut but the difficulties referred to earlier mean that the method is unlikely to be widely used.

According to Sizer (1989), SCRI recognised that publication counts provide relatively little information about the quality of publications and that citation analysis may be undertaken in three distinct contexts:

(i) when reviewing the provision of individual disciplines;

(ii) when undertaking periodic assessments of departmental performance, either externally by the UFC and Research Councils, or internally by an institution's Planning and Resources Committee and/or Research Committee;

(iii) as part of an annual series of management statistics and PIs.

SCRI's 1989 consultative document *Issues in Quantitative Assessment of Departmental Research* suggested that citations analysis is 'a partial indicator of the impact of the published output of research, and is capable of generating a variety of useful measures such as citations per paper, number of highly cited papers, numbers of uncited papers'. However, various difficulties were stressed including the delay before the citations record of a paper becomes apparent and the reduced relevance to those disciplines where the typical form of published output is not a paper in a refereed journal. It was there 'open to discussion whether the insights generated by citations analyses are worth the effort and cost of collecting and analysing data'. It seems very unlikely therefore that SCRI will be incorporating citations data into the management statistics and PIs, especially as the responses to the consultative exercise revealed much scepticism about citations analysis.

In its Report of the 1989 research selectivity exercise the UFC was even more dismissive of citations analysis and suggested that the SEPSU study undertaken for the UGC led to the conclusion that 'there was little to be gained by the use of citations counts and, more broadly, that bibliometric analysis was as yet a very poor substitute for peer review' (paragraph 30).

There have been some studies (for example Collins and Wyatt 1988) showing how citations to patents could form a PI for more applied research.

4.4 Research Income

The data needed to compute research income are readily available from USR returns and so it comes as no surprise that the 1987 CVCP/UGC statement on performance indicators lists research income per full-time equivalent staff member as one of the indicators to be included in the 1987 list. However, the use of research income in this way raises a number of difficult issues. Some kinds of research in all disciplines are less dependent on research income than others. In many cases, more abstract and theoretical work, which often is accorded the greatest prestige, is not so dependent on research income as work requiring experiments or the collection and analysis of large amounts of data.

Secondly, the process of getting and implementing research contracts diverts academics from what might be more rewarding research activities. There is thus a risk that maximisation of research contract income may promote pedestrian or even routine activity. It can be argued, of course, that success in gaining research contracts, especially in attracting 'repeat purchases', is a sign of relevance or success in the market place, but this view must be tempered by a recognition that many of the benefits conferred by research activity are spread over many individuals or organisations, and not restricted to those which fund it. The 'market' test may thus be an inappropriate measure of a project's value.

One may view the allocation of funds as the outcome which results from departments competing in the market for research income. Viewed in this light the allocation of research income may tell us something about the relative efficiency of the competing products, ie the research from different departments. At the same time, research income is an input into the research production process, and should be taken into account in evaluating research productivity.

Using research income as a measure of relative product competitiveness exploits the economic concept of market share. Perhaps the best example of this type of assessment and one which provides a useful analogy for our purposes is that of the competitiveness of UK products relative to the rest of the world. One way of assessing the UK's relative competitiveness is to look at UK market share of world exports.

In a very crude sense, the country with the greatest share of world exports is producing the most competitive products, as demonstrated by consumer preferences. As a direct analogy the relative competitiveness of research may be indicated by the willingness of the awarding body to provide funds. The best products therefore obtain the most research income, and as a result the level of research income allocated to a department may be taken as a measure of its relative competitiveness. There are, however, three important qualifications to this line of argument.

First, it is important to adjust for department size. In terms of our analogy with measuring the relative competitiveness of UK products on world markets, it would clearly be unreasonable to expect the UK to have as large a share of world exports as the USA - simply because the USA has more resources and is therefore able to produce a larger proportion of world output. Similarly, large departments can produce a great deal of research and as such are likely to take a larger share of total research income. When judging performance on the basis of research income obtained it is necessary to make some adjustment for the amount of resources available for obtaining the research income.

However any adjustment must avoid ambiguities. For example, departments which are successful in gaining research contracts use the revenue to engage research staff. Standardising for department size by dividing research income by total staff (including those supported by research grants) would be a false measure of the energy and success with which research contracts are sought, because as fast as research funds are added to the numerator, the denominator is increased by the employment of more staff. A more satisfactory approach is required which relates research income to the number of centrally-funded full time equivalent staff in a department, thus measuring their success *per capita* in attracting research grants. An appropriate basis for this variable is provided by the return of academic staff to the USR, whether the latter are defined as those employed either for teaching and research or for research only, and who are funded only from General Funds. There may, in addition, be a case for weighting the two categories of teachers and researchers differently.

The second and related point is the nature of economies of scale in the production of research. Unit costs may vary with department size. If there are economies of scale in the production of research - ie if output increased more than proportionately for every increase in resources - this would imply that large departments have a relative cost advantage over smaller departments. Large departments may therefore appear to be performing more efficiently than smaller departments by taking a larger share of total research income than their size might otherwise dictate. Naturally this situation is reversed if there are diseconomies of scale.

This presents a problem in interpreting market share since some departments may be constrained in size in the short run. In the long run, one might expect the forces of competition to generate an equilibrium in the research income market allowing departments to adjust to their optimum size. Once this has occurred market share becomes a more appropriate measure of product competitiveness. If there are no economies or diseconomies of scale then market share will not be distorted by relative cost advantages. Furthermore, identifying those departments who take the largest market share as being the best does not identify those departments who would produce the most from increased resources. Diseconomies of scale would imply that giving greater research income to smaller departments would produce a larger increase in research output than applying the same increase to a larger research department.

Finally, there are many different sources of research income. The data discussed below, taken from the UGC annual returns, distinguish eight sources - grants from research councils, research contracts, grants from industry and commerce etc. The degree of 'competition' differs in each of these markets. Many view grants from research councils as the most prestigious, and they always have the potential of generating publishable research results which will be picked up in research output indicators, whereas research contracts often lead to 'closed' reports. It is thus important to distinguish between sources of income as well as the aggregate amount.

The use of research income as an indicator of research performance, as was the case in the 1986 UGC research selectivity exercise, has attracted wide criticism (see for example, Gillett 1989; Hare and Wyatt). Gillett (1989) listed 15 defects in indices based on research income 'the cumulative effect of which is that the predictive validity of grant-giver peer review is likely to be extremely low' (p.26). Some of the main criticisms include that it is an input measure that provides no information about the quality and quantity of research produced; there are a number of structural factors in the great allocation scheme which create the 'illusion of validity' of funding decisions; there is an unmerited twofold advantage to grant holders who, with research assistants, ought to be able to produce more papers; departments which concentrate their research effort in areas where grants are in short supply, or the research is comparatively inexpensive are discriminated against; and inefficient departments might be rewarded and cost effectiveness ones penalised.

At the SPSG seminar Sizer defended the use of research income in the 1986 UGC exercise and claimed, for example, that information was provided by research councils on research funded which was considered unsatisfactory and research proposals which were alpha rated but remained unfunded.

Concern was also expressed that in the 1986 exercise sub-committee assessors gave more weight to grants from research councils and charities than to contracts from industry as measures of performance. This operated against more technologically orientated departments with close links with industry. Based on the information (quoted in Chapter 4.1) from the Circular Letter 45/88 Anderson concluded the 'UGC now make it clear that no distinction is expected' (p.148).

The 1989 UFC Report on the selectivity exercise shows that the way research income was taken into account was not entirely in line with the impression created in Circular 45/88. The Report states that the research income data were 'of considerable importance to the Science, Technology and Medical Panels but of no real significance, even where it existed, for the Arts/Humanities, and of only very limited significance in the Social Sciences. In the main greater weight was given to grant income especially from the Research Councils, and less weight to industrial and commercial contracts' (paragraph 25).

The Report later justifies the greater emphasis given to Research Council grants on the grounds that the focus of the UFC's 'science research funding is towards basic and strategic work; for more applied research, universities are expected to seek funding from other sources, both public and private . . . Given that the assessment process concentrated very much on the academic quality of published work, it naturally followed that departments with high outputs of good quality pure science scored more highly than departments with a largely applied science bias' (paragraph 38).

It is not surprising, therefore, that there was some initial criticism of the 1989 research selectivity exercise from the technological universities (*Times Higher Education Supplement*, 8 September 1989) with Professor

Ashworth, Vice-Chancellor of Salford University suggesting the results reflected the criteria used as much as performance. If it was the original intention of the UFC to give greater attention to grants than contracts, it would have been better had this been made clear in Circular Letter 45/88, rather than the impression created that the bias against applied research in the 1986 exercise was going to be corrected. Furthermore, the bias against applied research to some extent runs contrary to the PIs being developed for the Research Councils which stress the importance of collaboration with industry and income being gained by research establishments from the private sector (Cave and Hanney 1990).

The 'very limited significance' given to research income in the social sciences is also a matter for concern to those who share with the Chairman of the Economic and Social Research Council, Professor Newby, a belief in the importance of field work and data collection in the social sciences.

In the first edition of this book we calculated an index of performance based on research and contract income for a natural science cost centre, physics and human science cost centre, psychology. The aim was to show that the ranking of departments by research income is highly sensitive to whether research income is measured absolutely or on a per capita basis. We also showed that there existed a fairly weak relationship between research income adjusted for department size and the 1986 UGC ranking.

We adopted a similar general approach to analyse the relationship between research and contract income and the UFC evaluations of 1989. A simple regression of the UFC research grading on research income per full-time staff member was carried out for the 14 cost centres at Brunel University. It showed that the relationship is significant (as measured by standard statistical tests) in 10 of the 14 cases, the exceptions being Other Biological Sciences, Materials Technology, Education and Other Social Sciences. However, only in four of the 10 cases where a statistically significant relationship exists is the relationship strong in the sense that research income *per capita* contributes substantially to the research grading. These four cases were: General Engineering, Physics, Electrical Engineering and Chemistry. When staff numbers were introduced as an additional independent variable, the same general pattern was maintained, although not surprisingly the explanatory power of the equation increased.

Thus in general the relationship between the research rankings and research income adjusted for department size does not appear to be strong. One might have expected income from research contracts and grants to have provided a stronger positive relationship with the rankings since one would expect research grants to be allocated to those departments which the UGC/UFC considers best.

Earlier we argued that the basis for using research income as a performance indicator is that in essence research income is a measure of market share and that relative market share may provide information about the competitiveness of the 'firms' in the market. There is however an alternative interpretation. In this second view, research grant and contract income is seen as an additional input into an institution or department. This extra input should be reflected in higher output. On this view, high research and contract income creates the expectation of more output and the evaluation should be reduced for those producers who fail to achieve better results. There is evidence that some UGC Sub-Committees adopted this approach, and this may contribute to the explanation of the weak relationship between research rankings and research grant and contract income in many cost centres.

4.5 Peer Review of Research

Peer review of research is difficult to define precisely and can be considered to include a variety of activities. Gillett (1989) suggests 'peer review' is a generic term which includes impressionistic peer review, grant giver peer review, and journal peer review. In this section, however, we are concentrating on the first of these categories which is what is most commonly understood by peer review. The decision to include peer review in a list of PIs is controversial. Clearly it is not a straightforward PI and in many ways forms a higher tier being a judgemental process based to varying degrees on the other PIs. As in other sections consideration is given here to both the nature of the indicator and the way it has been used in the UK. As Chapter 1.1 explains, peer judgements made on a reputational basis have traditionally been the major form of evaluation used by the UGC. The move towards PIs can be seen as implicitly representing a weakening of trust in peer review - a move towards displacing evaluation by peers with evaluation by methods that managers rather than academics can master and control. However, the use of PIs can also be seen as a way of informing, and thus strengthening, peer review. Sizer has consistently argued that PIs should help narrow the gap that has to be bridged by peer judgements and claims that 'peer review and performance indicators should, and must, complement each other' (1990, p.25). Similarly Anderson (1989) shows how several Visiting

Committees involved in peer review of AFRC establishments generated their own bibliometric indicators to assist them. He describes the role of indicators in 'democratising' research funding in several Research Councils by improving the transparency of the resource allocation process by making it more open and visible to both the donors and recipients of funds.

Paradoxically, whilst the move towards PIs could be seen as reducing the significance of peer review, the financial and reputational impacts of the peer judgements made in 1986 and 1989 have been more severe and controversial than many previous ones. At the same time the current moves towards more systematic evaluation have had an impact on the nature of peer review. The more peer judgements become systematic and based on general criteria, the more appropriate it might be to describe them as being a PI, but, the less appropriate it might be to describe the process as being peer review as it has been traditionally understood.

The 1986 statement of the CVCP/UGC Working Group suggested that peer review was a PI but, in making that observation, it did not distinguish between PIs for research and for teaching. The Working Group defined peer review as being 'assessments of departments by individuals or groups who are acknowledged experts in the field of study.'

There is a sense in which peer review is applicable to individuals as well as departments. Some of the other PIs listed by the Working Group, for example, being an officer of a learned society or a member of a research council, can be seen as being based on peer review of individuals. This illustrates the point made by the Working Group that 'various aspects of peer review are hidden in others of the proposed PIs'. Although the Working Group did not mention them, the number of departmental staff with prizes, honours, and/or membership of bodies such as the Royal Society or the British Academy, can also be regarded as a PI based on peer review of the research of individuals. A list of esteem indicators along the above lines is being developed by SCRI. In the United States this is regarded as important in a number of multi-dimensional lists and provides a quantifiable indicator that can be used to compare departments. Peer review of the research of individuals and departments is also present in decisions about research grants and applications and the publication of journal articles, which have been discussed earlier in this chapter. Peer review of individuals also plays a major part in decisions about promotion.

Peer review of departments, it can be argued, should involve the following: those being reviewed knowing who are the reviewers; the reviewers getting to know the full range of the work of those being reviewed; those reviewed having the opportunity of being interrogated on their work so that misunderstandings can be adjusted and the reviewers become more knowledgeable about that which they are judging. It can also be argued that peer review ought to mean review by 'genuine' peers who are not too different in status from those being reviewed and yet are experts in the field being reviewed. The CVCP/UGC Working Group cites UGC Sub-Committees as an example of bodies already practising peer review; these disappeared, however, with their parent body.

It can be questioned whether the ranking of departments and institutions created as a result of subjective peer review and traditionally adopted by the UGC Visiting Committees should be considered to be a PI, as we define it in Chapter 1. A UGC statement implied that traditional peer review did not produce PIs when they stated that 'research can be assessed through peer judgement and a variety of PIs' (UGC, 22/85). If PIs are defined, however, as attempts to provide indicators through ordinal rankings for items that are not directly quantifiable, then peer review could be thought of as a PI.

The relationships between the UGC Visiting Committees and the allocation of resources by the UGC was not made clear before they embarked on the grading exercise. The distinction between peer review of teaching and of research was not made. Perhaps this distinction was not relevant at a time when the funding decisions were taken by the UGC Sub-Committees on the basis of what has been described as 'informed prejudice' (Moore 1987), and there was no attempt to develop a formula under which the contributions of the varying elements could be considered.

By 1986 the decisions of the UGC Sub-Committees had become more systematic and authoritative. The process was referred to as 'peer assessment' by Harris, a member of the UGC and as 'informal peer review' in the 1989 UFC Report. Criticisms of it have, however, been raised. The 1986 process did not meet the definition of peer review offered in the previous paragraphs and Zander, indeed, referred to it as a 'spurious peer review'. Critics also suggested that the 1986 process was unsystematic and 'riddled with flaws, with prejudice and with circularity of argument' (Chartres 1986).

The central problem, however, in treating products of the UGC process as PIs lies in the difficulty of the coalescing of UGC peer review for the assessment of departments with UGC peer review as the authoritative judgement about the resources to be received through the JR element of the grant. The latter judgement is based on a consideration of factors beyond peer judgement. In the 1986 UGC exercise the Sub-Committees made their assessments on the research departments according to a formula which included an important element of peer judgement. Those concerned with the development of PIs, especially the CVCP/UFC Steering Group, do not argue that PIs can ever totally replace judgement. Rather, they suggest, PIs can inform the judgements. This makes the place of peer review - especially when conducted by those with the authority to make the final judgement - rather ambiguous when compared with other PIs.

Gillett suggested that impressionistic peer review does not provide a true PI because there is currently no meaningful way to link impressionistic peer review with any input measure. He went on to suggest that if each of the PIs employed in the 1989 research selectivity exercise were to be combined into a single rating, then a mechanical weighting scheme would be preferable over a judgemental one. He cited psychological research to support the view that 'the predictive validity of a mechanical formula is almost always superior to that of a judgemental approach' (p.37). Whilst most academics would be likely to reject this, there is perhaps a growing interest in exploring ways in which quantitative and qualitative evaluation can be combined. There were several discussions on this at the 1988 CIBA Foundation Conference on the Evaluation of Scientific Research (Evered and Harnett, eds 1989). It is an issue of growing interest across the board in evaluation studies.

The lack of clarity about the position of peer review emerged again in the list of criteria to be used in the 1989 exercise. In this list in Circular Letter 45/88 (quoted in Section 4.1) professional knowledge and judgement was itemised as one of the four main criteria to be used in the whole process which was again described as informed peer review.

A major example of the use of peer review alongside that of bibliometric indicators has been the techniques of 'converging partial indicators' developed by Martin and Irvine at SPRU and referred to earlier (see, for example, Martin and Irvine 1983). They believed that traditional peer review was subject to limitations. A complex procedure was devised in which the research output and impact of a centre were compared with those of matched equivalents in other countries, with input figures being used to construct productivity and performance measures. Structured interviews were used to produce peer-rankings and in many cases showed 'a strong association exists between bibliometric data and expert judgement' (Irvine 1989, p.143).

More formal reputational rankings than those used earlier by the UGC have sometimes been considered to be a category of peer review. Such rankings are based neither on visits nor discussion by a small group. Instead, a large number of experts, for example heads of department, are asked to rank the departments in a particular subject across the nation. Some of the major American examples of reputational rankings were discussed in Chapter 2.2. An example in the UK is the rankings organised by the *Times Higher Education Supplement*, although these have been criticised as being limited in coverage and crudely interpreted by the journalists who published them. Such rankings are not always limited to a consideration of research, although this is the field for which they are probably most suited. It is easier and more appropriate to convert reputational rankings into a quantifiable PI than it is to convert the other forms of peer review but there are various problems with them. Complaints have been made that reputational rankings lack objectivity and are over influenced by tradition and the size of a department. Thus Crewe (1987) found that reputational rankings on political science were more closely correlated with departments' total output than with output *per capita*. Reputational rankings may do less than justice to departments straddling disciplines, or with many specialist sub-divisions, unless care is taken to include explicit judgements on them all. There is also a danger of a halo effect (Jones 1982; Fairweather 1988) whereby departments may benefit unduly from the reputation of the whole institution.

In America extensive use is also made of peer review of the more traditional types. The reviews can be carried out on individuals for decisions such as promotion or tenure and can be conducted by, for example, internal committees, external referees, or all the other members of staff, either in committee or by the completion of questionnaires. The research of the individual being reviewed need not be the major factor taken into account, although this will depend on the type of institution. Similarly, as we saw in Chapter 3.7 frequent use is made in America of peer review for purposes of accreditation but, again, research is only one of many factors taken into account.

In 1986 the CVCP/UGC Working Group appeared to anticipate that peer review of research would involve a visit by external reviewers because it suggested that it would probably only be used as a 'selective mechanism to probe more deeply into a particular department when other performance indicators suggest that there may be problems or causes for concern'. Several departments which were dissatisfied with the 1986 assessment of their research asked for a peer review exercise to be conducted on their research. The 1989 UFC Report made clear, however, that this was considered to be prohibitively expensive and time consuming.

If some of the difficulties can be overcome, and appropriate ways developed for using peer review as a PI, evaluation by peer review offers considerable attractions to academics, as being the PI most in keeping with traditional academic norms. An alternative use of peer review of research as a PI could be, as was suggested for peer review of teaching, to see whether it is practised and used in a formative way to improve the performance of the department. The 1989 UFC Report claimed that many thought the principal purpose of research assessment should be to guide departments towards improving their research performance. It commented: 'this, of course, was never the principal objective of either assessment exercise - the intention has been to fund areas of identified strength, not to identify areas of weakness and to advise on their improvement' (paragraph 41).

The use of peer review as a PI of research is, we have seen, criticised from several angles. At a theoretical level it is argued that peer review, if conducted in the full sense of an interactive review by visiting peers, can never be sufficiently systematic to be regarded as a PI. However, even when full visits are carried out there can be strong criticisms made that they fail to capture the unique qualities of the research being assessed.

Kogan and Henkel's (1983) analysis of the peer review of DHSS-funded research units carried out by the Office of the Chief Scientist reveals several potential problems with peer review. In various ways the people selected to carry out the review could be inappropriate. For example, they might be too senior to be regarded as peers or they might be insufficiently specialist in the subject studied by the research unit. In multiple funded units there is a danger of reduction of evidence and the assessment of the unit as a whole could be arbitrary. The basis on which the review is to be conducted - for example, purely scientific merit or a mixture of scientific merit and policy relevance - might not be clear. The adversarial mode adopted for such visits, whatever its merits, might not be appropriate for fields of research where there is insufficient consensus about the criteria for evaluation, and the result might be not a wholly rational or objective assessment but rather one in which adversarial skills rather than scientific ability are tested. Finally, insufficient attention might be given to the complexities of group judgements, especially when the group contains a member who might be attempting to perform before his colleagues. Elton (1980) showed how a peer review of a unit for which he was responsible posed a threat because of the interrogative rather than consultative mode in which it was conducted.

Many of the points raised by Kogan and Henkel are likely to apply widely to peer review conducted by means of visits. The 1986 UGC assessments of research did not directly involve visits, although previous visits could have had some impact on the peer judgements made. An attempt was made to make the process more systematic than it had been in 1981 and earlier years. This was done by means such as asking each cost centre to submit a three page profile of its research and nominate five research publications typical of the best produced by the cost centre. The opinions of others including the research councils and appointed assessors were sought to augment the judgements of the UGC Sub-Committee members themselves.

Other criticisms have been made of the 1986 exercise. The UGC grant allocation exercises have probably never been sufficiently interactive to enable the whole process to be regarded as a satisfactory peer review. The 1986 exercise, however, failed to achieve the standards of 'verifiability, freedom from bias, and quantifiability' that would have made them acceptable as PIs. Phillimore, having set out the full list of desirable characteristics for PIs contained in the 1986 CVCP/UGC Working Party Report, comments 'it is not unfair to say that the UGC exercise in 1985-6 singularly failed to meet any of these criteria with the indicators it purportedly used' (p.266). A former Chairman of the UGC is reported as saying that, as usual, the UGC had got it 80% correct. Chartres (1986) said of the 1986 exercise that 'while the basis of advice has been more open and perhaps less imprecise, assessment based on a combination of research income and 'judgement' is essentially the same as in the past'. As in 1981 the exercise can be criticised on the grounds of lack of consistency in criteria, anonymity and incomplete data. The exercise in no way met the criteria set out above for proper peer review; had it done so the costs involved would have been very high.

In 1986 the UGC ranking exercise was opposed by a majority of academics according to a poll conducted for the *Times Higher Education Supplement* (5 June 1987). Questions have been raised, however, about the extent to which even the inadequate procedures laid down were followed. Zander suggests that it would have been impossible, in the time available, for the members of the UGC Sub-Committees to have read the five publications submitted by each cost centre. There are also suggestions that some cost centres submitted more evidence than the UGC requested and so different centres were considered on different grounds. The names of the people who acted as assessors or who provided additional information to the UGC Sub-Committees were not known.

Just as it is difficult to differentiate between the peer review process and the procedure used to decide the JR element for each university, so equally it is hard to distinguish between criticisms of the whole selectivity exercise in 1986 and 1989 and the criticisms of the peer review element. Given, however, that the whole process was referred to as 'informal peer review', it seems reasonable to include all the criticisms here. Compilations of the criticisms of the 1986 exercise were reported by Smyth and Anderson and by Phillimore. In the 1989 Report the UFC listed nine main criticisms about the 1986 exercise:

(a) the criteria for assessing research quality had not been made clear to universities;

(b) the identify of assessors, whose advice had been sought, had been withheld;

(c) evaluation of research on the basis of UGC cost centres/ university departments had not allowed proper assessment of the work of inter-disciplinary research groups and of joint departments;

(d) the information sought from universities had biased judgements in favour of larger departments;

(e) the descriptive terminology in announcing the ratings was confusing; 'below average' had been understood to imply a low absolute standard;

(f) different assessment standards had been used for different subjects;

(g) the exercise, being retrospective, had taken little account of work in progress and research potential;

(h) there had been no appeals mechanism against particular ratings; and

(i) there had been insufficient consultation with subject and professional groups.

In view of the earlier discussion it is perhaps significant that the UFC did not list some of the major criticisms noted by others including the alleged bias against applied research. The considerable steps taken by the UFC to overcome some of these problems in the 1989 exercise were described in Section 4.1. Certainly compared with 1986 it seems fair for the UFC Report to say of the 1989 exercise; 'the level of criticism of the exercise has been muted' (paragraph 19). It discussed some of the criticisms that were made and the extent to which they could be overcome in any future selectivity exercise. It noted that the section of the questionnaire on staff members was 'needlessly complex and confusing' (paragraph 22) and that on publications 'caused problems of definition for some universities' (paragraph 23). The composition of some of the advisory groups and panels caused concern: 'the extent to which work by, say, younger researchers in the smaller universities would be known to and properly understood by older senior staff from the larger, more prestigious universities is at least for consideration' (paragraph 33).

Criticism of the cost of the 1989 exercise was anticipated and was therefore estimated by means of a survey of eight universities. The total cost was thought to be £4.1 million, most of which was 'opportunity cost'. Some of the Report's other points were referred to earlier including: the discrimination against applied research; the very limited extent to which the exercise was formative; the extent to which the exercise was retrospective and underplayed the opportunities to demonstrate attempts at future improvement; and the unreliable nature of some of the publications data. The Report stated that the numerical totals of publications were not found to be helpful 'and featured very little in the assessment process . . . the data were considered to be too unreliable and, where reliable, said nothing about quality of output' (paragraph 23). The assessment panels did rely heavily on the publications data, but on the qualitative rather than the quantitative aspects. It was admitted that there was insufficient time to read the two items nominated by each staff member, but at least the procedure was an improvement on the five publications per cost centre allowed in 1986. As Phillimore noted, critics of the 1986 exercise advocated greater use of publications data. Such critics might reasonably have anticipated more use of numerical data about publications. With respect to publications data, and to research income - especially research contracts - the impression was created by the criteria set out in Circular Letter 45/88 that the peer review process would be informed by quantitative data to a greater extent than turned out to be the case.

The subjects where there has been most criticism of the 1989 exercise include those in the humanities and social sciences. Historians, for example, according to the *Times Higher Education Supplement* (1 December 1989), were critical of the use of bibliometrics. The analysis above suggests that, if anything, too little use was made of quantitative indicators. The other main point made by the History at the Universities Defence Group, and some other subject groups, is that the singling out of research for evaluation created an absurdly one-sided view of the work of academics. Their argument that teaching should also be assessed was shown in Chapter 3 to be an increasingly widely shared view.

Uncertainty about how far the 1989 research selectivity reflected the quantitative data received makes it difficult to assess the statistical analysis conducted by Johnes and Taylor (1990a) on the results of the exercise. Their main findings were, first, that large departments appear to have a better chance of obtaining a high research rating than small departments, and, second, for half the cost centres included in their analysis, the research ratings were significantly related to the mean research ratings of other cost centres within the same institution. They propose alternative explanations of the latter finding. It does suggest that the halo effect was at work, but it is also consistent with a competitiveness effect, whereby the competition for resources within institutions is a powerful inducement for individual cost centres to improve their research performance. The interpretation of the first finding is more problematic. Johnes and Taylor suggest that 'there is substantial evidence that research performance benefits from scale economies, particularly (but not exclusively) in the sciences'. Although they admit their results are preliminary and should treated with caution, it can be seen that this conclusion disagrees with evidence referred to in Chapter 4.2 which questioned the existence of economies of scale in research. Furthermore, the general discussion in this section and in 4.2 demonstrates the possibility that unless peer review or reputational ranking is strongly informed by quantitative data, there is an inevitable tendency for there to be a bias in favour of larger, and therefore usually, better known, departments. It could be argued that it would only be appropriate to draw the conclusion that the findings demonstrate the existence of economies of scale, if it were known that quantitative data about research output had strongly influenced the 1989 exercise.

The UFC will again conduct a consultative exercise in 1991 before the next research selectivity exercise. According to the *Times Higher Education Supplement* (26 October 1990), changes to be considered will include a redefinition of the list of acceptable research publications. One aim of the changes will be to ensure that the treatment of research in the arts is appropriate.

Summary

By contrast with the assessment of teaching, the evaluation of performance and research is widely seen as providing a more acceptable focus for the use of PIs.

This chapter has described the methods adopted by the UGC/UFC in its adjudication on research status. These constitute a gradual introduction of PIs into resource allocation. The use of output measures such as publications, licenses and patents were then reviewed. Until recently, such work was mainly based on US experience, but partly by way of reaction to the UGC research rankings alternative British research output measures have now been published. We then discussed the problem of identifying quality or impact through an adjustment of quantitative measures, noting the use of citations indices and the difficulties associated with them. Research and contract income as a performance indicator has the advantage of readily available data but, again, the problems associated with its use are formidable.

Finally, we discussed the relationship between peer review and performance indicators. We reported criticisms of the use of peer review and identified possible ways in which it can be developed. In recent years subjects like physics and chemistry have faced successive subject review, selectivity ratings and the SCRI publications pilot study. As was reported with regard to assessment of teaching in America, there is an air of evaluation fatigue within the university community. Although the various exercises were conducted for different objectives, there is as strong a case in research as there is in teaching for the development of an authoritative set of PIs which could then be used for a number of purposes. Always providing, that is, that the objectives of the evaluation are compatible with those of institutions to which they are being applied.

Chapter 5

Types and Models and Modes of Application

5.1 Review of our Selection of Performance Indicators

Before making our own proposals for the use of performance indicators we should summarise our criticism of those published in 1987 by the CVCP and UGC. Because of data limitations and time constraints, the CVCP and UGC initially limited themselves mostly to the publication of comparative cost data. These are useful in triggering off questions about an institution's performance, especially in undergraduate teaching, but they do not represent any advance in the measurement of quantity or quality of output. They can be criticised on the grounds that they are mainly addressed to the problem of controlling costs - which is a vital objective, but not the most intractable problem facing higher education. Institutions are being pressed by government to assess the quality of their outcomes, and particularly those of research, in the hope of improving them. Once institutions and departments can be sure what they are producing they can better decide their priorities. These objectives will not be met by following the indicators originally put forward by the CVCP and UGC for immediate application, though the latter may yield some limited information on costs and we have noted continuing but slow progress since 1987 in improving the indicators produced by the CVCP and UFC. We have also noted encouraging developments in the PCFC sector.

Performance indicators have a potential role at several levels of the higher education system. These can be broadly grouped into two major categories - at the level of the funding body, which gains funds from the Government and makes inter-institutional comparisons, and the level of the institutions, where detailed planning, budgeting and accounting exercises are performed. These uses place different requirements on the indicators, in terms both of content and of level of aggregation; these differences are discussed below.

The indicators on teaching and research which we have identified from the literature as applicable are as follows:

(A) Relating to Teaching:

(1) Entry qualifications

(2) Degree results

(3) Cost per student or staff-student ratio

(4) Value-added

(5) Rate of return

(6) Wastage and completion rates

(7) Employment on graduation

(8) Student and peer review

(B) Relating to Research:

(1) Number of research students

(2) Output of research

(3) Quality or impact indices

(4) Research incomes

(5) Peer review

(6) Reputational rankings.

It is useful to classify and evaluate these performance indicators according to a number of criteria. We propose to adopt the following:

(1) Type of Indicator

Is the indicator a measure of input, output, productivity or final outcome? Is it a simple quantity index, or is it adjusted for quality?

(2) Relevance

How accurately does the performance indicator measure true underlying performance, relative to the organisation's given objectives?

(3) Ambiguity

Is it possible to identify a high or a low value of the indicator as unambiguously favourable or unfavourable? This may seem a minimum requirement, but it is not hard to cite instances where it is not met. For instance, a high cost per student can be interpreted either as a sign of wasteful extravagance or of the giving of more individual attention.

(4) Manipulability

If a performance indicator can be manipulated by the individual or body which it is intended to assess, its value is reduced. For example, numbers of research students can be inflated if selection is undiscriminating.

(5) Cost of Collection and Availability of Comparative Data

Some performance indicators can be calculated readily from data already available to institutions or the higher education system. Others require costly and perhaps infeasible data collection. For many purposes, comparative data are required, because the department's performance compared with others in the same field is a better guide than its absolute level.

(6) Level of Aggregation

Each performance indicator has its own natural level or levels of aggregation - individual, department, discipline, institution or the higher education system as a whole. They may thus be correspondingly difficult to bring together or weight.

(7) Relation to Other Indicators

Often several indicators are used to measure the same or a similar aspect of performance. In such circumstances, the existence of multiple indicators is a useful consistency check, but these variables should not be regarded as independent in an overall evaluation. In other cases a single indicator, for example number of research students, measures several dimensions of activity.

Table 4, at the end of this chapter, gives a preliminary evaluation of the characteristics of the 14 indicators listed above, based upon the more detailed discussion in Chapters 3 and 4. Thus, indicator 1, 'entry scores', is a measure of input quality, recording the strength of demand for places. Yet a high entry score does not of itself unambiguously denote good performance because, taken in conjunction with some levels of final degree results, it may indicate low added value. The indicator can also be manipulated. On the other hand, it is cheap to collect and process on a comparative basis.

Cost of Performance Indicators

The cost of collecting and using performance indicators has not been fully investigated either here or elsewhere, although the high costs of evaluating education more generally have been analysed (for example, Alkin and Solmon 1983). In cases where data are already collected by the UGC, the marginal cost of preparing them for use as performance indicators is small. This consideration has virtually dictated the coverage of the CVCP/UGC list of indicators published in 1987 although the 1989 gradings exercise cost about £4 milion. For other indicators, only occasional estimates of cost of collection are available. Some writers have properly maintained that an indicator should be used only when the benefits from its use exceed the costs. But there are problems in making a cost-benefit appraisal indicator by indicator. These arise in part because of jointness of costs - for instance publication and citation data are often conveniently collected together. More fundamentally, the return to developing performance indicators in higher education is not simply the summation of returns to individual indicators, but rather the overall effect of the total process. A single indicator may be subject to strategic manipulation which can be prevented by use of another related indicator. Equally the use of indicators across the board may trigger a change in attitudes to resource management not realisable by small-scale experiments.

Uses of Performance Indicators

We have already noted in Chapter 1 a conventional distinction in the literature on performance indicators between the objectives of economy (avoidance of over-spending), efficiency (productivity) and effectiveness (attainment of objectives). Operationally, because of measurement difficulties - particularly of quality of output - such simple distinctions become blurred. It is not clear, for instance, whether a given cost increment illustrates waste or the attainment of higher quality output. In any case, at any time an institution or an evaluation programme has a range of objectives to which any given performance indicator will be linked to a greater or lesser extent.

Thus an evaluation in which performance indicators play a part may have a range of possible aims. Pollitt identifies 10 purposes of performance assessment schemes but highlights how the interests of the consumers are often not paramount (1987; 1988). Evaluation may be used to raise questions about the organisation of resources, or to clarify objectives. Alternatively, it may be closely tied to improving resource allocation, given a clearly specified set of objectives. For example, given an output target for graduates in Russian, a funding body may seek the least costly way of meeting it. Here resources follow measurement more directly. Klein and Carter (1988) suggest PIs may be used as either 'dials' or 'tin openers'. If they are the former, measuring accurately the inputs, outputs and processes of higher education, they can be used to regulate the supply of resources directly. If they are the latter, their function is to identify issues requiring further examination. The process may be more formative than summative, and be intended to provide feedback on performance to the members of an institution without necessarily affecting resource availability. Again, such data may be used in assessments of individuals. The indicators will play different roles and receive different priority in each of these cases.

Moreover, the ranking of objectives will vary over time. This is partly a question of changes in preferences. It is indisputable that in major US universities the importance attached to teaching, both in the assessment of individuals and of departments or institutions, has declined substantially in the past 50 years. A similar process may be occurring in the UK where increasing importance is being attached to scholarly output *per se*, and to the role of research in meeting the needs of the economy. In other cases a funding body may take the view that inefficiency in some areas - for instance the allocation of research equipment or of student numbers - is so glaring that it makes sense to concentrate on eliminating it, even at the cost of neglecting other performance measures. Higher education is not as immutable as either its critics or admirers believe.

Indicators may also be used to measure trends rather than levels and this is an approach favoured in the US by Miller (1987). For this reason it is often useful to have data covering a series of years, and to look at changes over that period. As well as reducing the effect of measurement error or of anomalous results in particular years, this procedure makes it possible, when used with caution, to discern deterioration or improvement. It not only identifies future problem areas but also enables resources to be allocated on the basis of forecast as well as recorded performance.

The relationship between PIs and the use of judgement is complex. We observed in Chapter 2.3 how in Holland PIs can be seen as a way of providing an incentive to make the qualitative reasoning more precise. PIs play a role in increasing the transparency and accountability of decision taking. But using PIs as an aid to judgement raises a weighting problem: how much weight should be given to the numbers and how much to the judgements, especially in cases where the two diverge? In practice, the weighting problem is often resolved in favour of judgement, but the additional data made available can influence and sometimes justify the judgement. Collecting and presenting PIs need not always strengthen the hands of managers and information collators: the effect is sometimes, paradoxically, to strengthen the role of professional judgement rather than to weaken it. For instance in the UFC's 1989 research selectivity exercise final judgements were made by expert sub-committees. These were to some degree protected from criticism by the data collection exercise which preceded them, despite problems with that exercise which the UFC itself acknowledges. The potentially complementary roles played in quality assessment by PIs and qualitative approaches, including peer review, are subject to considerable analysis (see, for example, Allsop and Findlay 1990; Goedegebuure et al 1990).

The weight to be given to expert judgement and the importance of errors and ambiguities in the measures vary with the level at which the data are used. Within the framework of managing higher education, at least five areas of use can be discerned: in dialogues between the Treasury and the Department of Education and Science, between the DES and the funding bodies, between the funding bodies and institutions, within the institutions, and within departments.

These introductory remarks have identified some of the general problems which arise in developing and using performance indicators. They have emphasised the variety of indicators and the variety of purposes to which they can be put. We hope that they will also explain our choice of indicators and the considerations which might apply to their use. They further justify the need for institutions not slavishly to follow formulae created by others but to make their own choices of the indicators that will serve their purposes best.

We now turn to two areas of application in particular - the use of performance indicators by funding bodies to decide allocations among institutions, and their use within institutions to make assessments of faculties or departments. Before doing so, however, it should be noted that a non-funding body, the CNAA, believes that they should provide a strengthening of quality assurance processes (CNAA 1990).

5.2 Use of Performance Indicators by Funding Bodies

The focus of this study is on the institutions themselves, but our observations yield certain conclusions relevant chiefly to the funding bodies. The funding bodies have always made judgements without reference to the detailed problems of particular institutions. Such procedures were not particularly harmful in the past when growth was emphasised and where there were reasonable margins within which inequities and uncertain judgements could be absorbed. However that situation has now changed. Moreover, as noted in Chapter 1, the successful implementation of a system of performance indicators requires careful attention to a framework which should include identifying the relevant objectives of the organisation, specifying the level or parts to which the indicators will be applied, listing the indicators to be used, and devising strategies for their application and predicting the implications that they might have.

In the past, the UFC has used performance indicators as a major element in resource allocation in the following sense. Allocations are divided between teaching and research. Funds allocated to each university for teaching are based on planning numbers by cost centre and category (undergraduate or postgraduate); these are compiled by the UGC on the basis of data provided by the universities. The institution's grant for teaching is the sum of allocations to all of its cost centres, where each cost centre has a particular cost per student uniform across all universities. At the same time, the student numbers on which the allocation is based are determined by planning totals agreed between the university and the UFC.

The procedures for research allocations as recently elaborated have been set out in Chapter 4. They consist of a basic level of provision, an element dependent on income from research councils and private foundations and from contract research, and an element based on academic judgement. Finally, a small proportion of the UFC allocation is based on special factors. It is now, however, intended to transfer progressively research funding to the research councils.

The allocation system is thus based heavily on performance indicators - *ex ante* targets in the case of teaching, *ex post* evaluations in the case of research. In 1990 the innovation was introduced of specifying separately for each cost centre its research and teaching allocation.

Viewed in the light of the previous discussion, the system has a number of weaknesses:

(1) The performance indicator used to allocate resources for teaching is insufficiently specified and indiscriminate because it is based on a given cost per student uniform across all institutions. The discretionary aspect operates primarily through the allocation of planning numbers to universities, but the criteria of allocation are not clear. There is no sign of systematic collection of evidence or of any attempts to compensate for - for example - relatively low levels of attainment of entering students. In short, a performance indicator is used with no explicit quality correction; quantities are chosen on the basis of unspecified criteria.

(2) For research allocations, an explicit attempt has been made to allocate resources on the basis of performance, but the procedures used initially in 1985 were attacked within the higher education system, where they were widely perceived as inadequate and unfair. The procedures based on the 1989 exercise were regarded as an improvement.

(3) Little attempt has been made to understand or take account of the processes underlying teaching and research. On the one hand, it is important to reward good performance; on the other it may be efficient to move resources at the margin to poorer departments where they might cause improvement.

There is nothing inherently wrong in making allocations to higher education on the basis of separate evaluations of teaching and research, although neither inputs into nor outputs of either can be identified rigorously. But there is considerable scope for improving the performance indicators for each, for refining the process of using them and for disclosing their basis and mode of application. Broadly this would involve:

(a) for research, developing more comprehensive measures of performance, including those of a quantitative kind. The funding body should be prepared to devote more resources to compiling data on (i) quantity of research output; (ii) research income; and possibly (iii) quality or impact (citation rates) of research. This would involve the development of standard practices for reporting output, and the expenditure of some resources (though only a fraction of those devoted to research). Nonetheless it is likely to provide a more satisfactory quantitative base for the subsequent application of other forms of appraisal, including peer judgement. Such data bases can be prepared only centrally, and should be available to the institutions for the purpose of internal evaluation. It is not unreasonable to spend a proportion of the total expenditure of a programme on monitoring and evaluation. Within higher education at present, such expenditures are negligible. The developments, described in Chapter 4, being initiatied by SCRI should mean that by the time of the next research gradings exercise each university should have a publications data base using a standardised format, and there should be some data on research output in the annual volume of PIs;

(b) for teaching, the funding body should consider whether it wishes to introduce more diversified and complete indicators for use in resource allocation. The combination of setting grants to institutions and 'advising' on numbers in broad subject areas fails to make resource allocation transparent. It is not clear how or why institutions are rewarded financially for teaching, or how planning totals are determined. A better approach is to identify more clearly the relationship between student numbers and teaching allocation. Allocations per student need not be constant over all ranges of output and they could be differentiated in accordance with performance where appropriate indicators are available, but they should be disclosed. This is not to deny that the development of such indicators will be difficult. At the same time, if criteria such as the recruitment of students with non-standard qualifications are in operation, then they should be enunciated and a reward system established for them. At the very least, if the development of differentiated allocations per student is not possible, there should be a clearer link between perceived teaching quality and the number of student places allocated;

(c) indicators for both research and teaching as discussed in (a) and (b) above would be a starting point for the funding bodies' appraisal of institutions and their departments. It would be dangerous and unfair, however, to rely upon them without recourse to other information. They cannot, of themselves, say anything about the varying contexts in which academics work. Only visitations involving careful observation and discussion with the relevant parties can do that. Nor can they take full account of changing potential although an attempt to do this was incorporated into the 1989 research selectivity exercise. They essentially depend upon recent history, projections from which have limited usefulness. Far more detailed interrogation would be necessary to take note of changes in ethos, staffing and institutional behaviour, all of which will affect future performance. In scrutinising the publications record of a department it is important to take account of those who are active there at the time that the judgement is being made. The potential of those moving in needs to be taken into account and the achievements of those moving out need to be discounted, at least to some extent. The capacity of a group of academics to learn from previous evaluation might be a further subjective criterion. What have they done since the previous evaluation? Have they listened to the encouragements and the warnings given then?;

(d) a further issue is that of the quality of the evaluative process. In principle, it should be capable of withstanding a judicial review if the resulting judgements were challenged in a court of law. Judicial reviews conducted on behalf of those contesting decisions of local education authorities have succeeded when it has been shown that those affected by a decision have not been given an adequate opportunity to inform themselves of its consequences and to make adequate representation. Whilst the judgements of funding bodies are not bound by statutory procedures, they certainly ought to be transparent to all of those affected by their outcomes and they should give the opportunity for full justifications to be heard, for corrections of fact to be made and, perhaps, for judgements to be disputed;

(e) our final difficulty with the present system (the apparent absence of any model of the processes of teaching and research) is concerned more with the overall structuring of higher education than with performance indicators as such. The Government, the Advisory Board on Research Councils and the UFC have recently proposed or adopted decisions on the restructuring of higher education, especially in the field of research. However, these discussions have largely taken place outside the performance indicators debate, and without systematic empirical evidence on the productivity or efficiency of different types of institution. The funding bodies appear to dissociate the restructuring issue from that of providing appropriate success criteria and incentives for institutions in their current states.

We noted in Chapter 2 that a more fundamental review of ways of assessing performance in teaching has been undertaken by the Morris Committee set up by the PCFC (Morris 1990), that they proposed a public expenditure compact with the DES, that PIs should be linked with the corporate planning process and the setting of objectives and that the income and expenditure profile of institutions should be based on information from an inter-institutional comparison service.

The Morris Committee has thus established a considerable agenda for the use of performance indicators by the PCFC. It carries moreover the interesting implication that the proposed system will provide some check on the DES' performance. It creates the expectation that the DES must be clear about the objectives which it sets for higher education and should provide a means by which the system's performance, for which the DES is accountable, should be assessed.

It is clear, however, that the PCFC's (and the UFC's) approach to performance indicators must be made congruent with other changes which are taking place in the finance and control of higher education. We noted in Chapter 1 the introduction by the PCFC of a limited degree of competitive tendering for student places for 1990/91. The operation was repeated on a slightly diferent scale for 1991/92. At the same time the UFC sought bids for all student places for the period from 1991/92 to 1994/95.

Despite the UFC's disappointment at the limited amount of price competition which it elicited from the universities in their tendering process, it is likely that some kind of bidding or tendering system for higher education is here to stay. It is thus important to consider how the introduction of this additional factor may change the requirements imposed upon performance indicators. One of the key problems with tendering is the risk that some institutions may tender too low a price, and then find themselves obliged to cut the quality of provision in order to avoid the risk of bankruptcy.

Higher education is not, of course, the only part of the economy exposed to competitive tendering. It has been commonplace in the private sector for centuries. Local authorities have been subject to competitive tendering since 1979, and aspects of the recent health service reforms involve competition between suppliers through a tendering process. In some of these cases contracts are awarded solely on the basis of price; in others on a combination of price and quality.

There is little doubt that competitive tendering has lowered the price at which services are provided in a range of public sector activities. Most of the debate about its effects has revolved around the quality of service. Demonstrating that quality has fallen or remained constant is a difficult task, but it is in the logic of competitive tendering that the contracts go to the cheapest providers. These may either be the most efficient, or those most capable of adapting the letter of the contract to their advantage, or those most adept at resisting contract enforcement.

The higher education tenders are different in structure from the simpler cases of bidding, as they fix not only the price at which transactions are made, but the quantities too. Both demand and supply can respond independently to price, with the funding body adjusting the number of, say, physics places it buys according to the price it has to pay, and the institutions through their tenders varying the amount which they are collectively willing to supply as the price varies.

With knowledgeable and sophisticated tenderers, a process of this kind might be expected to yield efficiency gains. Institutions would have a chance to specialise in those activities where they have a cost advantage or a quality advantage. But there must be doubts about whether higher education institutions are in fact capable of behaving in this way. Most institutions have very little idea of the costs they incur in teaching students in different subject groups, partly because they lack adequate accounting systems, and partly as a result of genuine problems in allocating costs which are common among different activities (such as teaching and research) or among different disciplines. In such circumstances institutions may be prey to a version of the fallacy of competition. They see that one more student can be added to any given number at a low marginal cost, for instance by adding him or her to an existing tutorial group or making all the students queue one second longer to get out of the library. This argument is then applied successively to larger increases, in a way which ignores the need ultimately to take on an additional tutor or librarian or to add a new wing to the building. Believing the fallacy tends to promote variable bidding, as exemplified by the wide dispersion of bids reported by the PCFC. When the cost pressures bite, the institutions will be under pressure to lower quality, which is any case hard to monitor.

It is noteworthy that the PCFC has made a particular effort to identify certain programmes of 'outstanding quality' and to reward the institutions providing them by favouring their bids for places (PCFC 1990). The Council also employed a 'moderation factor' to limit the rate of growth which might otherwise have been attained by institutions tendering low prices per student in the 1990/91 exercise. Thus an explicit attempt was made both to reward quality and to limit the risk of quality degradation to which the tendering process might otherwise lead, and to preserve some institutions tendering at very low rates from the consequences of their actions. This approach, combined with the gradual introduction of tendering by the PCFC, seems calculated to generate some of the efficiency gains from the process while avoiding some of the more obvious risks.

But the general point remains that the growth of tendering in higher education increases the requirements placed upon performance indicators in the sector because it brings institutions into direct competition with one another on price. This makes the proper monitoring of teaching quality still more important.

In summary, the proposed new procedures for tendering for higher education places do not address many of the difficulties with the present system noted above. Instead they sharpen the need to introduce some of the more sophisticated procedures we have suggested in this section. Unless the appropriate steps are taken, tendering may have an adverse effect on quality.

5.3. Use of Performance Indicators within Institutions and Departments

The greatest opportunities for performance indicators - and the greatest problems - arise at the level of institutions and departments, and the use of performance indicators at these levels is being urged in many systems, whether central control is becoming stronger or weaker. As noted in Chapter 2.3, the Swedish authorities have encouraged institutional or faculty or departmental self-evaluation as a means of reinforcing decentralisation. A similar motive, within a rather different policy framework, can be noted in the Netherlands where, because of its dominance in the funding and direction of higher education, central government was 'the focal point of institutional behaviour' (Dochy, Segers and Wijnen 1987). The change in relationships with the state has led to attempts to introduce systematic quality control but with the government applying it globally and *ex post*. But this is believed to reinforce the need for institutional and sub-institutional self-evaluation. According to Kells (1986), 'significant, internally initiated institutional study, planning and change processes are increasingly encountered at US institutions.' We have already noted the Morris Report's recommendations to the PCFC that performance indicators should form part of a corporate attempt to strengthen institutional self-evaluation and development, and hence autonomy. It is to be hoped that their expectations are met although it must be noted that many defences of the introduction of performance review start with the same ambitions. The CNAA has explored ways in which PIs can be used to assist institutions in conducting self appraisals (CNAA 1989).

No matter what the policy setting, however, institutions must allocate resources fairly so that activities are well maintained and incentives are provided for further development. They cannot afford to deal in abstractions but must be able to justify their judgements in detail.

We consider here, therefore, how far performance indicators might be used both to allocate resources and as a means of educating and guiding members of institutions.

Performance indicators, covering both teaching and research, can, if they are adjusted for quality, help to achieve both purposes. Nobody will claim that any indicator on its own is an adequate measure of performance. Used together, however, a range of performance indicators covering teaching and research might provide a quantitative picture of a department's performance relative to such reference groups as equivalent departments in other institutions.

Within institutions, performance indicators are to be used within the framework of a management system for the allocation of resources; the UFC expects them to govern allocation of research funds within universities. According to the Jarratt Report, the key role in such a system should be played by a planning and resources committee, comprising members of the university's Senate and Council, responsible for identifying and achieving strategic objectives. Such a committee will have the task of evaluating the institution's portfolio of research and teaching activities, setting budgets, establishing control processes and evaluating outcomes.

Our concern is with the role of performance indicators in this process. If they are to be used as an input in the allocation of resources, they must then be factored into procedures leading to a wider ranging evaluation. A picture derived from rather crude performance indicators would not meet the total needs for evaluation.

What might move an institution from the relatively simple task of computing performance indicators to the achievement of a broader evaluation? Once the performance indicators have been found, each department would be invited to consider how accurately they record costs and outcomes and how far they fail to disclose the true picture of performance. As already noted, the performance data might well strengthen rather than weaken the professional judgements. Also they could draw attention to contextual factors affecting performance which the institution should bear in mind before administering rewards, incentives or punishments. This process would help departments to clarify their objectives and to provide a running and reiterative critique, leading to improvement of the performance indicators. It would also help institutions to formulate weightings, which would probably change over time, for different aspects of performance. These would not be uniform across departments, but would be made explicit.

In determining what weightings to allow, institutions will face the key issue of how to promote marginal effects. For incentive reasons, resources should be directed to high achievers. Yet they may be most productive at the margin in low-performing departments, with, for example, tired and discouraged staff.

It is also the case that, at the level of the individual staff member, performance indicators can play an equivalent but necessarily more 'formative' role. But that will depend on whether they are used mechanistically or sensitively and with a due degree of negotiation about the consequences of their use.

If, then, institutions are to measure output, to identify those departments which can make the best use of extra resources and to allocate them accordingly, two types of PIs can be broadly defined. There are those which measure some aspect of cost and those which provide more or less informal measure of performance. Each of these two types of indicators is discussed in turn.

Indicators of Cost and Output

We noted in Chapter 3 that average cost data have to be interpreted with caution, both because departments and institutions vary in quality of output and because of special factors (for example, inherited staff or buildings) which may unavoidably raise costs. There is also the problem of establishing uniform accounting procedures across institutions.

Nevertheless, institutions would be unwise to neglect average cost data entirely. When presented in disaggregated form, as in the CVCP/UFC compilation of management statistics and performance indicators, they identify cases in which expenditure on particular items (for example, telephones or maintenance) falls outside the normal range. More generally, data on average cost per student in a particular cost centre should raise questions. If unusually high, are they compensated by high quality of output (including research output) in the relevant cost centre, or explained by extraneous factors? If unusually low, are they the result of exceptional efficiency or at the expense of other aspects of performance? Institutions also may wish to consider comparing their performance against a subset of organisations in similar circumstances - for example, of the same size or type. It should be possible to provide such comparisons instantly and to identify issues requiring explanation. We would not, however, recommend an automatic policy of regression to the mean.

In sum, therefore, institutions might take account of several forms of information. They need to compare their costs with comparable costs in other institutions. For these, they will need access to data bases created and made available by funding bodies. Secondly, they need output data for research, and we have suggested above what these might be. Thirdly, as far as teaching is concerned, institutions might use judgements made by students, evaluations made by peers through external examining or through visiting committees, or, indeed, external inspection - perhaps instigated at the request of the institutions themselves. Chapter 3.2 showed how a value-added approach might be useful to institutions as part of their quality assurance process. Finally, much of their best information will come not through the route of performance indicators but by rigorous interaction with the departments which, when faced with 'objective' data, will soon enough begin to produce a mass of information relevant to their assessment which otherwise might have lain dormant.

Use of Peer Review

This leads us to consider the role of peer review, which might mitigate the crude application of performance indicators and contribute towards developmental evaluation.

In Chapter 4 we attempted to identify the main functions that peer review of research might achieve. We elaborate those points here and take up questions of process. Interactive peer evaluation, through visits which should follow adequate assessment of the range of research and teaching undertaken, can move beyond the documentation of figures already provided by PIs and make two further kinds of judgement. First, irrespective of the quantities, is something good or bad happening in a department and institution? The process should be open, and the identity of the evaluators should be known. They should hold themselves open to interchange with those whom they are evaluating. Secondly, in making the judgement, they can take account of contexts. This may mean acknowledging that it is not so easy to undertake research if a great library is not near to hand, or that multiple objectives are being pursued because an institution is under pressure; but credit should be given for work completed all the same. The evaluation need not imply that an unfavourable context will result in further resources being made available. It could, indeed, lead to the conclusion that the unit being evaluated cannot fulfil its functions properly, albeit through no fault of its own. But contexts are important and are not easily captured by numerical PIs.

Use for Self-Evaluation

Whilst our discussion has concentrated on the use of performance indicators for the purpose of resource management by the system and by the institutions, we have indicated that we regard the use of performance indicators, and other modes of evaluation, as relevant and potentially useful to the exploitation of self-knowledge by the departments themselves.

Examples of attempts to inaugurate self-evaluation can be found in Sweden, Australia and the Netherlands and are briefly noted in Chapter 2.3. Those responsible for the Swedish initiative emphasised that it is intended to stimulate and foster critical self-study, that it should not be prescribed or ordered from above (Furumark 1981). The experiments vary widely in orientation. Some are based on a rationalist approach and aimed at potential products rather than at improving the process of self-evaluation itself. The products are then used primarily outside the self-studying units. There are also other, non-bureaucratic, aims of self-evaluation.

One documented UK attempt (Sizer and Frost 1985) tests a procedure enabling departments to develop a profile of research and scholarship. The project was intended to encourage departments to evaluate their own research by developing and keeping up to date a profile of both the nature of the research and the types of outputs, benefits and impacts it produced. A paper on criteria to be used in evaluating research profiles was provided to departments to help identify the most relevant performance indicators for their type of research.

In considering the use of departmental profiles, the project noted the problems of peer evaluation in considering departmental profiles while also noting that it was 'relatively quick and cheap and normally not too time consuming'. It was noted that peer review works best at project level and within a single subject area. Sizer suggests that more work is needed on the peer review system to represent the views of non-specialists who can cope with multidisciplinary fields 'with clear industrial-commercial pay-offs'.

The Loughborough project is a helpful attempt to show how departments might set about self-evaluation for use by themselves and their institutions. We have already referred to PCFC and CNAA proposals for developments in the use of PIs in this field. The Morris Report also noted a suggestion from the CNAA that one way in which PCFC might take quality into account in its bidding process could be by encouraging institutions to elaborate their self-evaluation processes as follows:

(a) a list of a minimum of five and a maximum of ten key indicators of quality of teaching and learning would be prepared; and

(b) institutions would be asked to self-evaluate their own provision in each programme against the key indicators of quality, using a five point scale similar to that used by BTEC and HMI.

Use of Inspection

In many areas of professional life different forms of inspection, often thought to be essentially interactive and subjective in style, are increasing in importance. The schools have always had large central and local inspectorates. The Health Advisory Service (although carefully eschewing the term 'inspection') and the Mental Health Act Commissioners apply similar methods to the health service. Social workers are liable to inspection by the Social Services Inspectorate and by recently created local authority Social Services Inspection Units. Public sector higher education and teacher education in both sectors are inspected by Her Majesty's Inspectors of Schools but, so far, the universities in general have been virtually free of inspection. They have opted for an Academic Audit Unit which will evaluate university procedures for quality assurance in teaching. We have noted the PCFC's decision to use HMI judgements in their funding procedures and the proposals of the Morris Report that HMI assessments should be incorporated into sectoral performance indicators.

Inspection can be used by funding bodies to examine the quality of teaching and of the institutional milieu. A potential development might be its use by institutions or departments as an aid to self-evaluation.

Why Stop at Institutions?

PIs and other forms of evaluation are coming into place for institutions and their component units. We suggest that similar developments might also be appropriate for the national authorities. As with institutions and departments, the intention would be developmental rather than punitive. Because national authorities have outcomes meaningful in terms only of the output of the institutions which they sponsor, many of the indicators would be those of process and concerned with determining the cost and efficiency of the procedure adopted. The competence of central planning bodies to collect and interpret information and to relate their formulation of objectives to social and economic needs and to the capacity of the system becomes increasingly important as the power of the centre increases.

Finally, we have proposals for further work in this area. Throughout this text we have pointed out problems and difficulties in creating PIs and further work on them is obviously required, as is fully acknowledged by the DES and CVCP. We are struck by the extent to which the university indicators do not sufficiently differentiate between the costs of teaching, research, other services and administration. It seems essential to develop an analysis which is broken down by function as well as, by discipline or cost centre. Such data will provide a basis for much more systematic studies of comparative efficiency using economic analysis widely applied in other sectors.

Further work, too, might be undertaken on the institutional and organisational aspects of evaluation. At present there are many evaluative bodies each using different evaluative modes for different purposes. Research on the different modes of evaluation which they apply, their knowledge base and their authority and impacts would help clarify the nature of the system.

Table 4. Characteristics of 14 Selected Performance Indicators

Indicator	*Type*	*Relevance*	*Ambiguity*
Teaching			
1. Entry qualifications	Quality of input	Measures strength of demand	High entry scores may imply low value-added
2. Degree results	Quality-adjusted measure of output	Measures central teaching function of higher education	Good degree results may reflect high entry scores or other inputs
3. Cost per student or staff-student ratio	Productivity measure (no quality adjustment)	Involves difficult problems of cost allocation	High cost per student may reflect higher quality of teaching and better output; staff-student ratio ignores complementary inputs
4. Value added	Input-adjusted and quality-adjusted output measure	Measures of net output can be combined with input data to generate 'productivity' indicator	Typically measured through differences in qualifications. Monetary value of such increases not available
5. Rate of return	Quality-adjusted productivity measure	Assumes optimal valuations of output, ignores consumption benefits	Both private and social returns can be computed; levels will normally differ
6. Wastage and non-completion rates	Measure of 'wasted inputs'	Identifies problems with process of selection or teaching	Ignores quality of students on entry: use discourages wider access
7. Employment on graduating or after five years	Measure of output 'quality'	does not capture long-term employment prospects or market value of employment	high employment rates on graduation may result from too short a period of search, and leads to poor 'job matching'
8. Student and peer review	Measure of output and process quality	Contains major elements of subjectivity	Difficulty of defining good teaching (eg avoidance of 'spoon feeding')
Research			
1. Number of research students	Input quality	Measures student demand	Corrections for department size and discipline necessary
2. Publications patents, etc.	Measure of quantity of research output	Problem of making research outputs commensurable: differences in practices across disciplines of sub-disciplines	Difficulty of weighting teaching and research staff in establishing per capita measure: ignores complementary inputs - should work be attributed to current location of research or institution where work was completed?
3. Research quality based on a) citation of publications or b) impact factors of place of publication	Quality adjusted output measure	Difficult to produce complete sample	a) Citing of mistakes or summary rather than original work; b) based on 'average' values
4. Research income	Measure of input and 'competitiveness'	Can be broken down by type of contract, eg research council commercial organisations, etc.	Problem of choosing appropriate standardisation for department size
5. Peer review	Quality-adjusted output measure	Contains major element of subjectivity	
6. Reputational ranking	quality-adjusted output measure	Contains major element of subjectivity	Problem of low response rate; may reflect historic performance

Manipulability	*Cost of collection*	*Level of aggregation*	*Relation to other PIs*	
Manipulable by, for example, concentration on entrants with non-standard qualifications	Already available on a comparative basis	Department, institution	Input into calculation of value-added	1
Number and degree class of graduates partly at the discretion of department or institution	Already available	Department, institution (corrected for subject mix)	Gross output measure for value-added indicator	2
Should be corrected by wastage rate to prevent excessive 'low quality admissions'	Already available	Department, institution (corrected for subject mix)		3
Form of test may distort teaching and marking patterns	Often involves resolution of major measurement and conceptual problems and longitudinal study	Department, institution	Related to rate of return difference between degree result and 'entry scores'	4
	Substantial, arising from need for longitudinal study	Discipline	Related to 'value-added' (as production measures)	
Subject to institutions own examinations procedure	Already collected	Department, institution	Links with 'number of research students'	6
Relies on institutional (unaudited reporting)	First destination currently collected; subsequent employment monitoring involves major expense	Department, institution	Element of 'rate of return' calculation	7
Manipulable through form of assessment given to students	Already done in some institutions, varies according to the method adapted	Individual teacher, department (?)		8
Admission policy at department's discretion	Already collected	Department	Related to non-completion rates	1
Encourages publication of 'low grade' research	Already collected in most institutions but practices differ (eg are non-refereed articles included?)	Department or individual	Related to 'research income'	2
Encourages 'citation circles'	a) Substantial, involving lag b) Impact factors available from citation sources	Individual, department	Quality adjusted for 'research output'	3
May encourage performance of academically 'valueless' research	Already available	Department	Input into research output	4
	Cost depends on frequency	Department, individual	Builds on or complements other PIs	5
Risk of collusion in anonymous questionnaires		Department		

References

Aaronson, S., (1975), 'The Footnotes of Science', *Mosaic*, Vol. 6, 23-27.

Abrami, R., (1989) 'How Should We Use Student Ratings to Evaluate Teaching', *Research in Higher Education*, Vol. 30, No. 2, 221-227.

Adams, A., and Krislov, J., (1978), 'Evaluating the Quality of American Universities: A New Approach', *Research in Higher Education*, Vol. 8, 97-109.

Adelman, C., (ed.) (1986), *Assessment in American Higher Education*, Office of Educational Research and Improvement, Washington.

Advisory Board for the Research Councils, (1987), *A Strategy for the Science Base*, HMSO.

Ahn, T., Charnes, A., and Cooper, W. W., (1988), 'Some Statistical and DEA Evaluations of Relative Efficiencies of Public and Private Institutions of Higher Learning, *Socio-Economic Planning Sciences*, Vol. 22, No. 6, 259-269.

Alkin, M., and Solmon, L. C. (eds.), (1983), *The Costs of Evaluation*, Sage Publications.

Allen, D., Harley, M., and Makinson, G., (1987), 'Performance Indicators in the National Health Service', *Social Policy and Administration*, Vol. 21, No. 1, 70-84.

Allsop, P. and Findlay, P., (1990), 'Performance Indicators as an Agent of Curriculum Change: Broadening the Base of HE', in McVicar, M. (ed), *Performance Indicators and Quality Control in Higher Education*, Portsmouth Polytechnic.

Anderson, J., (1989), *New Approaches to Evaluation in UK Research Funding Agencies*, Science Policy Support Group.

Ashworth, T., and Thomas, B., (1987), *The Influence of School Performance on University Performance in Economics*, Department of Economics, University of Durham.

Astin, A., (1982), 'Why Not Try Some New Ways of Measuring Quality?', *Educational Record*, Vol. 63, Spring, 10-15.

Astin, A., and Solmon, L., (1981), 'Are Reputational Ratings Needed to Measure Quality?', *Change*, Vol. 13, October, 14-19.

Audit Commission, (1985), *Obtaining Better Value from Further Education*, HMSO.

Audit Commission, (1986), *Performance Review in Local Government: Education*, HMSO.

Australian Vice-Chancellors' Committee, Australian Committee of Directors and Principals, (1988), *Report of the AVCC/ACDP Working Party on Performance Indicators*, Canberra.

Baker, K., (1986), Speech to CVCP Conference at Edinburgh, September.

Baker, K., (1987), Report in *Times Higher Education Supplement*, 6th February 1987, 1.

Baker, K., (1988), Speech reported in *The Times*, 5.10.88.

Barnett, R., (1988) 'Entry and Exit Performance Indicators for Higher Education: Some Policy and Research Issues', *Assessment and Evaluation in Higher Education*, Vol. 13, No. 1, Spring, 16-30.

Barrow, M., (1990), 'Techniques of Efficiency Measurement in the Public Sector', in Cave, M., et al., *Output and Performance Measurement in Government: The State of the Art*, Jessica Kingsley Publishers.

Bauer, M., (1990), 'Sweden', in Kells, H., (ed.), *The Development of Performance Indicators for Higher Education: A Compendium for Eleven Countries*, OECD.

Bayer, M., and Folger, J., (1966), 'Some Correlates of a Citation Measure of Productivity in Science', *Sociology of Education*, Summer, 281-90.

Becher, T., and Kogan, M., (1980), *Process and Structure in Higher Education*, Heinemann.

Becher, T., and Kogan, M., (1991, forthcoming), *Process and Structure in Higher Education*, 2nd edition, Routledge.

Beeton, D., (ed.), (1988), *Performance Measurement: Getting the Concept Right*, Public Finance Foundation.

Bell, J., and Seater, J., (1978), 'Publishing Performance: Departmental and Individual', *Economic Inquiry*, Vol. 16, October, 599-615.

Beyer, J., and Snipper, R., (1974), 'Objective Versus Subjective Indicators of Quality in Graduate Education', *Sociology of Education*, Vol. 47, 511-557.

Biglan, A., (1973), 'Relationships Between Subject Matter Characteristics and the Structure and Output of University Departments', *Journal of Applied Psychology*, Vol. 57b, 204-213.

Billing, D., (1980), Introduction, in Billing, D. (ed.), *Indicators of Performance*, The Society for Research into Higher Education.

Birch, D., Calvert, J., and Sizer, J., (1977), 'A Case Study of Some Performance Indicators in Higher Education in the United Kingdom', *International Journal of Institutional Management in Higher Education*, Vol. 1, No. 2, October, 133-142.

Birnbaum, R., (1985), 'State Colleges: An Unsettled Quality', in Cohen, A. et al, *Contexts for Learning: The Major Sectors of American Higher Education*, The National Institute of Education and the American Association for Higher Education.

Bligh, D., Caves, R., and Settle, G., (1980), 'A Level Scores and Degree Classifications as Functions of University Type and Subject', in Billing, D. (ed.), *Indicators of Performance*, The Society for Research into Higher Education.

Blume, S. S., and Sinclair, R., (1973), 'Chemists in British Universities: A Study of the Reward System in Science', *American Sociological Review*, Vol. 38, February, 126-138.

Bogue, G. E., (1982), 'Allocation of Public Funds on Instructional Performance/Quality Indicators', *International Journal of Institutional Management in Higher Education*, Vol. 6, No. 1, 37-43.

Bormans, M., Brouwer, R., In't Veld, R., and Mertens, F., (1987), 'The Role of Performance Indicators in Improving the Dialogue Between Government and Universities', *International Journal of Institutional Management in Higher Education*, Vol. 11, No. 2, 181-193.

Bourke, P., (1986), *Quality Measures in Universities*, The Commonwealth Tertiary Education Commission, Australia.

Bourner, T., and Hamed, M., (1987), *Entry Qualifications and Degree Performance*, CNAA Development Services Publications 10.

Boyer, E., (1985), 'Changing Priorities in American Higher Education', *International Journal of Institutional Management in Higher Education*, Vol. 9, No. 2, July, 151-159.

Boyer, E., (1989), 'Olivet Branches Out With Five Year Tenure, *Times Higher Education Supplement*, 9.2.89. p. 17.

Boys, C. J. and Kirkland, J., (1988), *Degrees of Success: Career Aspirations and Destinations of College, University and Polytechnic Graduates*, Jessica Kingsley.

Bradbury, D., and Ramsden, P., (1975), 'Student Evaluations of Teaching at North East London Polytechnics', in *Evaluating Teaching in Higher Education*, University of London, Teaching Methods Unit.

Brennan, J. and McGeevor, P., (1988), *Graduates at Work. Degree Courses and the Labour Market*, Jessica Kingsley.

Brinkman, P., (ed.), (1987), *Conducting Interinstitutional Comparisons*, New Directions for Institutional Research No. 53, Jossey-Bass.

Brinkman, P., and Tester, D., (1987), 'Methods for Selecting Comparison Groups', in Brinkman, P., (ed.), *Conducting Interinstitutional Comparisons*, New Directions for Institutional Research No. 53, Jossey-Bass.

Brown, S. J., and Sibley, D. S., (1986), *The Theory of Public Utility Pricing*, Cambridge University Press.

Bud, R., (1985), 'The Case of the Disappearing Caveat: A Critique of Irvine and Martin's Methodology', *Social Studies of Science*, Vol. 15, 548-553.

Cabinet Office, (1989), *Research and Development Assessment: A Guide for Customers and Managers of R and D*, HMSO.

Carnegie Council on Policy Studies in Higher Education, (1986), *Classification of Institutions of Higher Education*, Berkeley, California.

Carnegie Foundation for the Advancement of Teaching, (1984), *Faculty Survey*.

Carpenter, M., Gibb, F., Harris, M., Irvine, J., Martin, B., and Narin, F., (1988), 'Bibliometric Profiles for British Academic Institutions: An Experiment to Develop Research Output Indicators', *Scientometrics*, 14, 213-233.

Carswell, D., (1988), Letter to *Times Higher Education Supplement*, 18.3.88.

Carter, N., (1989), 'Performance Indicators: "Backseat Driving" or "Hands Off" Control?,' *Policy and Politics*, Vol. 17, No. 2, 131-138.

Cartter, A., (1966), *An Assessment of Quality in Graduate Education*, American Council on Education.

Cave, M., and Hanney, S., (1989), *Performance Indicators in Higher Education: An International Survey*, Department of Economics Discussion Paper, Brunel University.

Cave, M., and Hanney, S., (1990), 'Performance Indicators for Higher Education and Research', in Cave, M., et al., *Output and Performance Measurement in Government: The State of the Art*, Jessica Kingsley.

Cave, M., Kogan, M., and Smith, R., (1990), *Output and Performance Measurement in Government: The State of the Art*, Jessica Kingsley.

Chartres, J., (1986), 'Selectivity - The Latest Cuts', *AUT Bulletin*, September.

CIPFA, (1984), *Performance Indicators in the Education Service*, CIPFA Consultative Paper.

Clark, K., (1954), 'The APA Study of Psychologists', *American Psychologist*, 9, 117-120.

Clark, A., and Tarsh, J., (1987), 'How Much is a Degree Worth?', in *Educational Training*, Policy Journals.

Clayton, K., (1987), *The Measurement of Research in Higher Education*, University of East Anglia.

Clift, J., Hall, C., and Turner, I., (1989), 'Establishing the Validity of a Set of Summative Teaching Performance Scales', *Assessment and Evaluation in Higher Education*, Vol. 14, No. 3, Autumn, 193-206.

Cole, J., and Cole, S., (1972), 'The Ortega Hypothesis', *Science*, Vol. 178, 17, October, 368-375.

Collini, S., (1989), 'Publish and be Dimmed', *Times Higher Education Supplement*, 3.2.89.

Collins, P., and Wyatt, S., (1988), 'Citations in Patents to the Basic Research Literature', *Research Policy*, Vol. 17, No. 2, April, 65-74.

Committee of Vice-Chancellors and Principals - Steering Committee for Efficiency Studies in Universities, (1985), *National Data Study.*

Committee of Vice-Chancellors and Principals and University Grants Committee, (1986), *Performance Indicators in Universities: A First Statement by a Joint CVCP/UGC Working Group*, CVCP.

Committee of Vice-Chancellors and Principals, (1986), *Reynolds Report. Academic Standards in the Universities.*

Committee of Vice-Chancellors and Principals and University Grants Committee, (1987), *Second Statement by the Joint CVCP/UGC Working Group*

Committee of Vice-Chancellors and Principals and University Grants Committee, (1987), *University Management Statistics and Performance Indicators: UK Universities.*

Committee of Vice-Chancellors and Principals, (1987), *Review of the University Grants Committee (Croham Report)*, Cm. 81.

Committee of Vice-Chancellors and Principals and University Grants Committee, (1988), *University Management Statistics and Performance Indicators in the UK*, Second Edition.

Committee of Vice-Chancellors and Principals/Universities Funding Council - Performance Indicators Steering Committee, (1989), *Issues in Quantitative Assessment of Departmental Research*, UFC, London.

Committee of Vice-Chancellors and Principals/Universities Funding Council, (1989), *University Management Statistics and Performance Indicators in the UK*, Third Edition.

Committee of Vice-Chancellors Principals/Universities Funding Council, (1990), *University Management Statistics and Performance Indicators in the UK*, Fourth Edition.

Cook, S., (1989), 'Improving the Quality of Student Ratings of Instruction: A Look at Two Strategies', *Research in Higher Education*, Vol. 30, No. 1, 31-45.

Coulter, W., and Moore, A., (1987), 'Utilisation of Performance Indicators for Financing Higher Education at State Level in the United States. The Ohio Case', *International Journal of Institutional Management in Higher Education*, Vol. 11:2.

Council for National Academic Awards, (1989), *Towards an Educational Audit*, Information Services Discussion Paper 3.

Council for National Academic Awards, (1990), *Performance Indicators and Quality Assurance*, Information Services Discussion Paper 4.

Cox, W. M., and Catt, V., (1977), 'Productivity Ratings of Graduate Programs in Psychology', *American Psychologist*, Vol. 32, 793-813.

Cozzens, S., (1989), 'What Do Citations Count? The Rhetoric-First Model', *Scientometrics*, Vol. 15, 437-447.

Crewe, I., (1987), *Reputation, Research and Reality: The Publication Records of UK Departments of Politics 1978-1984*, Essex Papers in Politics and Government, No. 44, Department of Government, University of Essex.

Cuenin, S., (1986), *International Study of the Development of Performance Indicators in Higher Education*, Paper given to OECD, IMHE Project, Special Topic Workshop.

Cullen, B., (1987), 'Performance Indicators in UK Higher Education: Progress and Prospects', *International Journal of Institutional Management in Higher Education*, Vol. 11:2.

Daffern, P., and Walshe, E., (1990), 'Evaluating Performance in the Department of the Environment', in Cave, M., et al., (eds.), *Output and Performance Management in Government: The State of the Art*, Jessica Kingsley.

DES, (1985), *The Development of Higher Education into the 1990s*, Green Paper, Cmnd. 9524, HMSO.

DES, (1987), *Accounting and Auditing in Higher Education.*

DES, (1987), *Higher Education: Meeting the Challenge*, White Paper, Cm. 114, HMSO.

DES, (1987), *Changes in Structure and National Planning for Higher Education, Universities Funding Council*, Consultative Document, DES.

DES, (1987), *Changes in Structure and National Planning for Higher Education. Contracts Between the Funding Bodies and Higher Education Institutions*. Consultative Document, DES.

DES, (1987), *Changes in Structure and National Planning for Higher Education. Polytechnics and Colleges Sector*, Consultative Document, DES.

Department of Education and Science and Department of Employment, (1985), *Graduates and Jobs: Some Guidance for Young People Considering a Degree*, HMSO.

Dochy, F., Segers, M., and Wijnen, W., (eds.) (1987), *Quality Assurance in Higher Education*, Dutch Ministry of Education.

Dochy, F. R. J. C., Segers, M. S. R., and Wijnen, W. F. W., (1987), *Managerial Context of the Research Project, The Use of Performance Indicators as a Part of the New Steering Conception in the Netherlands*, (mimeo), Limburg University.

Dochy, F., Segers, M., and Wijnen, W., (eds.), (1990), *Management Information and Performance Indicators in Higher Education: An International Issue*, Van Gorcum.

Dowell, D., and Neal, J., (1982), 'A Selective Review of the Validity of Student Ratings of Teaching', *Journal of Higher Education*, Vol. 53, No. 1, 51-62.

Drew, D., and Karpf, R., (1981), 'Ranking Academic Departments: Empirical Findings and a Theoretical Perspective', *Research in Higher Education*, Vol, 14, No. 4, 305-320.

Edwards Report, (1988), *The Future of University Physics*, UGC, HMSO.

Egan, J., (1986), *Value-Added Testing and Measurement: Will it Save Higher Education From Its Critics?*, Paper Presented at the Value-Added Learning Conference, Empire College, State University of New York, 4-6 June.

Elton, L., (1980), 'Evaluation of an Institute for University Teaching and Learning', in Billing, D., (ed.), *Indicators of Performance*, The Society for Research into Higher Education.

Elton, L., (1984), 'Evaluating Teaching and Assessing Teachers in Universities', *Assessment and Evaluation in Higher Education*, Vol. 9, No. 2, Summer, 97-115.

Elton, L., (1987), 'UGC Resource Allocation and the Assessment of Teaching Quality', *Higher Education Review*, Vol. 19, No. 2, Spring, 9-17.

Elton, L., (1987), 'Warning Signs', *Times Higher Education Supplement*, 11.9.87.

Elton, L., (1988), Book Review, *Studies in Higher Education*, Vol. 23, 337-338.

Elton, L., (1988a), 'Appraisal and Accountability in Higher Education: Some Current Issues', *Higher Education Quarterly*, Vol. 42, No. 3, Summer, 207-229.

Evans, T., and Clift, R., (1987), Letter to *Times Higher Education Supplement*, 18.9.87.

Evered, D., and Harnett, S., (eds.), (1989), *The Evaluation of Scientific Research*, Wiley, (A CIBA Foundation Conference).

Ewell, P., (ed.), (1985), *Assessing Educational Outcomes*, New Directions for Institutional No. 47, Jossey-Bass, San Francisco.

Fairweather, J., (1988), 'Reputational Quality of Academic Programs: The Institutional Halo', *Research in Higher Education* , Vol. 28, No. 4, 345-355.

Feldman, K., (1988), 'Effective College Teaching from the Students' and Faculty's Point of View: Matched or Mismatched Priorities', *Research in Higher Education*, Vol. 28, No. 4.

Feldman, K., (1989), 'Instructional Effectiveness of College Teachers as Judged by Teachers Themselves, Current and Former Students, Colleagues, Administrators, and External (Neutral) Observers', *Research in Higher Education*, Vol. 30, No. 2, 137-168.

Fox, D., (1984), 'What Counts as Teaching', *Assessment and Evaluation in Higher Education*, Vol. 9, No. 2, Summer, 133-143.

Frackmann, E., (1987) 'Lessons to be Learnt from a Decade of Discussions on Performance Indicators', *International Journal of Institutional Management in Higher Education*, Vol. 11:2.

Frame, J. D., (1983), 'Quantitative Indicators for Evaluation of Basic Research Programs/Projects', *IEEE Transactions on Engineering Management*, Vol. EM-30, No. 3, August, 106-112.

Fulton, O., (1986), *Entry Standards*, Paper Presented to the Anglo- American Seminar on Quality Judgements in Higher Education at Templeton College.

Fulton, O., and Ellwood, S., (1989) *Admissions to Higher Education: Policy and Practice*, The Training Agency.

Further Education Unit, (1986), *Research Project 304 - Towards and Educational Audit: Feasibility Study*, Further Education Unit and the Association of Colleges of Further and Higher Education.

Furumark, A., (1981), 'Institutional Self-Evaluation in Sweden', *International Journal of Institutional Management in Higher Education*, Vol. 5, No. 3.

Garfield, E., (1970),'Citation Indexing for Studying Science', *Nature*, Vol. 227, 25 August 1970,, 669-671.

Garfield, E., (1977), 'The 250 Most-Cited Primary Authors, 1961-1975. Part II. The Correlation Between Citedness, Nobel Prizes and Academy Memberships', *Current Contents*, No. 50, December 12 1977, 5-16.

Garfield, E., (1979), *Citation Indexing: Its Theory and Application in Science, Technology and Humanities*, John Wiley & Sons, New York.

Gardner, D., (1985), 'Managing the American University', *International Journal of Institutional Management in Higher Education*, Vol. 9, No. 1, March, 5-12.

Gevers, J. K. M., (1985), 'Institutional Evaluation and Review Processes', *International Journal of Institutional Management in Higher Education*, Vol. 9, No. 2, July, 145-148.

Gibbons, M., and Georghiou, L., (1987), *Evaluation of Research: A Selection of Current Practices*, OECD, Paris.

Gillett, R., (1986), *Serious Anomalies in the UGC Comparative Evaluation of the Performance of Psychology Departments*, Paper from Department of Psychology, University of Leicester.

Gillett, R., (1989), 'Research Performance Indicators Based on Peer Review: A Critical Analysis', *Higher Education Quarterly*, Vol. 43, 20-38.

Glenn, N., and Villemez, W., (1970), 'The Productivity of Sociologists at 45 American Universities', *American Sociologist*, Vol. 5, 224- 252.

Goedegebuure, L., Maasen, P., and Westerheijden, D., (eds) (1990), *Peer Review and Performance Indicators*, Uitgeverij Lemma, Utrecht.

Green Paper, (1985), *The Development of Higher Education into the 1990s*, HMSO, Cmnd. 9524.

Hare, P., and Wyatt, G., (1988), 'Modelling the Determination of Research Output in British Universities', *Research Policy*, Vol. 17, 315-329.

Harris, G., (1989), 'Research Output in Australian University Research Centres in Economics', *Higher Education*, Vol. 18, 397-409.

Harris, M., (1986), *Judgements of Quality in Higher Education: The Role of the University Grants Committee*, Paper Presented to the Anglo-American Seminar on Quality Judgements in Higher Education at Templeton College.

Hicks, D., and Skea, J., (1989), 'Is Big Really Better', *Physics World*, December, 31-34.

Hölttä, S., (1988), 'Recent Changes in the Finnish Higher Education System', *European Journal of Education*, Vol. 23, No. 1/2, 91-104.

Hüfner, K., (1987), 'The Role of Performance Indicators in Higher Education: The Case for Germany', *International Journal of Institutional Management in Higher Education*, Vol. 11:2.

Hüfner, K., (1987a), 'Differentiation and Competition in Higher Education: Recent Trends in the Federal Republic of Germany', *European Journal of Education*, Vol. 22, No. 2, 134-144.

Hüfner, K., and Rau, E., (1987) 'Measuring Performance in Higher Education - Problems and Perspectives', *Higher Education in Europe*, Vol. 12, No. 4, 5-13.

In't Veld, R., Spee, A., and Tseng, H., (1987), *Performance Indicators in Higher Education in the Netherlands.* Paper presented at the OECD Conference on Education Indicators, Washington DC, 3-6 November.

Irvine, J., (1989), 'Evaluation of Scientific Institutions: Lessons from a Bibliometric Study of UK Technical Universities', in Evered, D., and Harnett, S., (eds.), *The Evaluation of Scientific Research*, Wiley, Chichester (CIBA Foundation Conference).

Jappinen, A., (1987), 'Current Situation Regarding the Development and Use of Performance Indicators in Finland', *International Journal of Institutional Management in Higher Education*, Vol. 11:2.

Jarratt Report, (1985), *Report of the Steering Committee for Efficiency Studies in Universities*, Committee of Vice-Chancellors and Principals.

Johnes, G., (1986a), *Determinants of Research Output in Economics Departments in British Universities*, University of Lancaster, Department of Economics, Discussion Paper.

Johnes, G., (1986b), *Research Performance Indicators in the University Sector*, University of Lancaster, (mimeo).

Johnes, G., (1988), 'Research Performance Indicators in the University Sector', *Higher Education Quarterly*, Vol. 42, No. 1, Winter, 54-71.

Johnes, G., (1990), ' Measures of Research Output: University Departments of Economics in the UK, 1984-1988', *Economic Journal*, Vol. 100, June, 556-560.

Johnes, G., and Johnes, J., (1990), *Measuring the Research Performance of UK Economics Departments: An Application of Data Envelopment Analysis*, Lancaster University Management School, Discussion Paper, EC/17/90.

Johnes, J., (1990), 'Determinants of Student Wastage in Higher Education', *Studies in Higher Education*, Vol. 15, No. 1, 87-99.

Johnes, J., (1990a), 'Unit Costs: Some Explanations of the Differences Between UK Universities', *Applied Economics*, Vol. 22, 853-862.

Johnes, J., and Taylor, J., (1987), ' Degree Quality: An Investigation into Differences Between UK Universities', *Higher Education*, Vol. 16, 581-602.

Johnes, J., and Taylor, J., (1989), 'Undergraduate Non-Completion Rates: Difference Between UK Universities', *Higher Education*, Vol. 15, No. 3. 209-225.

Johnes, J., and Taylor, J., (1989a), 'The First Destination of New Graduates: Comparisons Between Universities', *Applied Economics*, Vol. 21, 357-373.

Johnes, J., and Taylor, J., (1990), *Performance Indicators in Higher Education*, SRHE and Open University Press.

Johnes, J., and Taylor, J., (1990a), 'The Research Performance of UK Universities: A Statistical Analysis of the Results of the 1989 Research Selectivity Exercise', Discussion Paper.

Johnes, J., and Taylor, J., (1991), 'Non-Completion of a Degree Course and its Effects on the Subsequent Experience of Non-Completers in the Labour Market', *Studies in Higher Education*, Vol. 16, No. 1.

Jones, L. V., et al, (1982), *An Assessment of Research Doctorate Programs in the UA*, National Academy Press, 5 Volumes, Washington DC.

Johnston, R., (1989), 'Do You Use the Telephone too Much? A Review of Performance Indicators, Evaluation and Appraisal in British Universities', *Journal of Geography in Higher Education*, Vol. 13, No. 1, 31-44.

Jordan, T., (1989), *Measurement and Evaluation in Higher Education*, The Falmer Press.

Kells, H., (1983), *Self Study Process*, Macmillan, New York.

Kells, H. R., (1986), 'The Second Irony: The System of Institutional Evaluation of Higher Education in the United States', *International Journal of Institutional Management in Higher Education*, Vol. 10, No. 2, July, 140-149.

Kells, H., (1989), *The Inadequacy of Performance Indicators for Higher Education: The Need for a More Comprehensive and Developmental Construct*, Mimeo.

Kells, H., (ed.) (1990), *The Development of Performance Indicators for Higher Education: A Compendium for Eleven Countries*, Programme on Institutional Management in Higher Education, OECD.

Kingman Report, (1989), *Costing of Teaching*, Committee of Vice- Chancellors and Principals.

Klein, R., and Carter, N., (1988) 'Performance Measurement: A Review of Concepts and Issues', in Beeton, D., (ed.), *Performance Measurement: Getting the Concepts Right*, Public Finance Foundation.

Knudsen, D., and Vaughan, T., (1969), 'Quality in Graduate Education: A Re-evaluation of the Rankings of Sociology Departments in the Cartter Report', *American Sociologist*, Vol. 4, 12-19.

Kogan, M., (1989), 'The Evaluation of Higher Education: An Introductory Note', in Kogan, M., (ed.), *Evaluating Higher Education*, Jessica Kingsley.

Kogan, M., and Henkel, M., (1983), *Government and Research*, Heinemann Educational Books.

Laband, D., (1985), 'An Evaluation of 50 "Ranked" Economics Departments - By Quantity and Quality of Faculty Publications and Graduate School Placement and Research Success', *Southern Economic Journal*, Vol. 52, No. 1, 216-240.

Laurillard, D. M., (1980), 'Validity of Indicators of Performance', in Billing, D., (ed.), *Indicators of Performance*, The Society for Research into Higher Education.

Le Grand, J., and Robinson, R., (1979), *The Economics of Social Problems*, Macmillan.

Liebowitz, S., and Palmer, J., (1984), 'Assessing the Relative Impacts of Economics Journals', *Journal of Economic Literature*, March, 77-88.

Lindop Report, (1985), *Academic Validation in Public Sector Higher Education*, Cmnd 9501.

Lindsey, D., (1989), 'Using Citation Counts as a Measure of Quality in Science: Measuring What's Measurable Rather Than What's Valid', *Scientometrics*, 15, 3-4, 187-203.

Linke, R., (1990), 'Australia', in Kells, H., (ed.), *The Development of Performance Indicators for Higher Education: A Compendium for Eleven Countries*, OECD.

Maassen, R., (1987), 'Quality Control in Dutch Higher Education: versus External Evaluation', *European Journal of Education*, Vol. 22, No. 2, 161-171.

Maassen, R., and Van Vught, F., (1988), 'An Intriguing Janus Head: The Two Faces of the New Governmental Strategy for Higher Education in the Netherlands', *European Journal of Education*, Vol. 23, Nos 1/2, 65-76.

MacRoberts M., and MacRoberts, B., (1986), 'Quantitative Measures of Communication in Science: A Study of the Formal Level', *Social Studies of Science*, Vol. 16, 151-172.

Marsh, H., (1987), 'Students' Evaluations of University Teaching: Research Findings, Methodological Issues, and Directions for Future Research', *International Journal of Educational Research*, Vol. 11, 253-388.

Martin, B., and Irvine, J., (1983), 'Assessing Basic Research: Some Partial Indicators of Scientific Progress in Radio Astronomy', *Research Policy*, Vol. 12, 61-90.

Martin, B., Irvine, J., and Crouch, D., (1985), *Science Indicators for Research Policy in Bibliometric Analysis of Ocean Currents and Protein Crystallography*, Science Policy Research Unit, University of Sussex.

Mathias, H., and Rutherford, D., (1982), 'Lecturers as Evaluators: The Birmingham Experience', *Studies in Higher Education*, Vol. 7, No. 1, 47-56.

Mayston, D., (1985), 'Non-Profit Performance Indicators in the Public Sector', *Financial Accountability and Management*, Vol. 1, No. 1, 51-74.

McClain, C., Krueger, D., and Taylor, T., (1986), 'Northeast Missouri State University's Value-Added Assessment Program. A Model for Educational Accountability', *Journal of Institutional Management in Higher Education*, Vol. 10, No. 3, 252-271.

McMillan, J., (1988), 'Beyond Value-Added Education', *Journal of Higher Education*, Vol. 59, 564-579.

McVicar, M., (ed) (1990), *Performance Indicators and Quality Control in Higher Education*. Papers presented to an International Conference held at the Institute of Education (University of London) on 27 September 1989, Portsmouth Polytechnic.

Mertens, F., and Bormans, R., (1990), 'Background to the Development of a System of Performance Indicators in the Netherlands', in Dochy, F., et al, *Management Information and Performance Indicators in Higher Education: An International Issue*, Van Gorcum.

Mertens, P., (1979), 'Comparative Indicators for German Universities', *International Journal of Institutional Management in Higher Education*, Vol. 3, No. 1, 155-168.

Miller, R. I., (1986), 'A Ten Year Perspective on Faculty Evaluation', *International Journal of Institutional Management in Higher Education*, Vol. 10, No. 2, July, 62-168.

Miller, R. I., (1987), Correspondence with Prof. M. Kogan.

Miller, R. I., (1987a), *Evaluating Faculty for Promotion and Tenure*, Jossey-Bass.

Ministry of Education, Finland, (1986), Development Act.

Minogue, K., (1986), 'Political Science and the Gross Intellectual Product', *Government and Opposition*, Vol. 21, No. 4, 185-194.

Moed, H., et al, (1985), 'The Use of Bibliometric Data as Tools for University Research Policy', *International Journal of Institutional Management in Higher Education*, Vol. 9, No. 2, 185-194.

Moore, P., (1987), 'University Financing 1979-1986', *Higher Education Quarterly*, Vol. 41, No. 1, January.

Moravscik, M., (1986), 'Assessing the Methodology for Finding a Methodology for Assessment', *Social Studies of Science*, Vol. 26, 534-39.

Morris Report, (1990), *Performance Indicators: Report of a Committee of Enquiry Chaired by Mr Alfred Morris*, PCFC.

Moses, I., (1985), 'High Quality Teaching in a University: Identification and Description', *Studies in Higher Education*, Vol. 10, 76-86.

Moses, I., (1986), 'Student Evaluation of Teaching in an Australian University - Staff Perceptions and Reactions', *Assessment and Evaluation in Higher Education*, Vol. 11, No. 2, 117-129.

Moses, I., (1989), 'Role of Problems of Heads of Departments in Performance Appraisal, *Assessment and Evaluation in Higher Education*, Vol. 14, No. 2, Summer 95-96.

Murray, H., (1984), 'The Impact of Formative and Summative Evaluation of Teaching in North American Universities', *Assessment and Evaluation in Higher Education*, Vol. 9, No. 2, Summer, 117-132.

Muth, J., (1961), 'Rational Expectations and the Theory of Price Movements', *Econometrica*, Vol. 29, No. 6.

NAB, (1987), *Management for a Purpose: The Report of the Good Management Practice Group*.

Narin, F., (1987), 'Bibliometric techniques in the Evaluation of Research Programs', *Science and Public Policy*, Vol. 14, 99-106.

Neave, G., (1985), 'Elite and Mass Higher Education in Britain: A Regressive Model?', *Comparative Education Review*, Vol. 29, No. 3.

Neave, G., (1987), 'Editorial', *European Journal of Education*, Vol. 22, No. 2, 121-122.

Neave, G., (1988), 'On the Cultivation of Quality, Efficiency and Enterprise: An Overview of Recent Trends in Higher Education in Western Europe, 1986-1988', *European Journal of Education*, Vol. 23, Nos. 1/2, pp.7-23.

Nederhof, A., and Van Raan., A., (1989), 'A Validation Study of Bibliometric Indicators: The Comparative Performance of Cum Laude Doctorates in Chemistry', *Scientometrics*, Vol. 17, Nos. 5-6, pp.427-435.

Newby, H., (1990), 'New Answers to Searching Questions', *Times Higher Education Supplement*, 30.3.89.

Niemi, A. Jr., (1975), 'Journal Publication Performance During 1970-1974: The Relative Output of Southern Economics Departments', *Southern Economics Journal*, 97-106.

Niiniluoto, I., (1990), 'Finland', in Kells, H. (ed.), *The Development of Performance Indicators for Higher Education: A Compendium for Eleven Countries*, OECD.

Ory, J., and Parker, S., (1989), 'Assessment Activities at Large Research Universities', *Research in Higher Education*, Vol. 30, No. 4, 375-385.

Osborne, M. J., (1989), 'On the Marginal Cost of a Student in the Public Sector of Higher Education in the UK', *Journal of Further and Higher Education*, Vol. 13, No. 1, Spring, 55-65.

Oxburgh Report, (1987), *Strengthening University Earth Sciences*, UGC.

Page, E., (1987), Letter to *Times Higher Education Supplement*, 25.9.87.

Page, E., (1988), Letter to *The Times*, 8.10.88.

Pettifor, J. C., *Print Out*, Nottingham Polytechnic.

Phillimore, A., (1989) 'University Research Performance Indicators in Practice: The University Grants Committee's Evaluation of British Universities 1985-6', *Research Policy*, Vol 18, 255-71.

Phillips, D., (1989), 'Chairman's Remarks', in Evered, D., and Harnett, S., (eds.), *The Evaluation of Scientific Research*, Wiley, (CIBA Foundation Conference).

Phillips, D., and Turney, J., (1988), 'Bibliometrics and UK Science Policy', *Scientometrics*, Vol. 14, 185-200.

Pollitt, C., (1986), 'Beyond the Managerial Model: The Case for Broadening Performance Assessment in Government and the Public Services', *Financial Accountability and Management*, Vol. 2, No. 3, 155-170.

Pollitt, C., (1987), 'The Politics of Performance Assessment: Lesson for Higher Education?', *Studies in Higher Education*, Vol. 12, No. 1, 87-98.

Pollitt, C., (1988), 'Bringing Consumers Into Performance Measurement: Concepts, Consequences and Constraints', *Policy and Politics*, Vol. 16, No. 2, 77-87.

Pollitt, C., (1989), 'Performance Indicators in the Longer Term', *Public Money and Management*, Vol. 9, No. 3, Autumn, 51-55.

Polytechnics and Colleges Funding Council, (1989), *Recurrent Funding Methodology 1990/1. Guidance for Institutions.*

Polytechnics and Colleges Funding Council, (1990), *Recurrent Funding and Equipment Allocations for 1990/91.*

Polytechnics and Colleges Funding Council and Council for National Academic Awards, (1990), *The Measurement of Value Added in Higher Education.*

Porrer, R., (1984), *Higher Education and Employment*, Association of Graduate Careers Advisory Services.

Porter, A., (1977), 'Citation Analysis: Queries and Caveats', *Social Studies of Science*, Vol. 7, 257-267.

Pratt, J., (1989), 'The Context' in *Report of a Conference on Performance Indicators in Teacher Education*, Centre for Institutional Studies, Polytechnic of East London.

Psacharopoulos, G., (1985), 'Returns to Education:A Further International Update and Implications', *Journal of Human Resources*, Vol. 4, 583-604.

Rasmussen, P., (1985), 'A Case Study on the Evaluation of Research at the Technical University of Denmark', *International Journal of Institutional Management in Higher Education*, Vol. 9, No. 1, March, 58-66.

Reynolds Report, (1986), *Academic Standards in Universities*, Committee of Vice-Chancellors and Principals.

Rhodes, D. M., and Rumery, R. E., (1980), 'Student Reports as Indicators of Instructor Performance', in Billing, D., (ed.), *Indicators of Performance*, The Society for Research into Higher Education.

Robey, J., (1979), 'Political Science Departments: Reputations Versus Productivity', *Political Science*, Vol. 12, 202-209.

Rogers, B., and Gentemann, K., (1989), 'The Value of Institutional Research in the Assessment of Institutional Effectiveness', *Research in Higher Education*, Vol. 30, No. 3, 345-355.

Rogers, A., and Scratcherd, T., (1986), Letter to *Times Higher Education Supplement*, 7.11.86.

Roith Report, (1990), *Research in the PCFC Sector: Report of the Committee of Enquiry Appointed by the Council*, PCFC.

Roose, K., and Andersen, C., (1970), *A Rating of Graduate Programs*, American Council on Education.

Rutherford, D., (1987), 'Indicators of Performance: Reactions and Issues', *Assessment and Evaluation in Higher Education*, Vol. 12, No. 2, Summer, 94-104.

Rutherford, D., (1988), 'Performance Appraisal: A Survey of Academic Staff Opinion', *Studies in Higher Education*, Vol. 13, No. 1, 89-100.

Segers, M., Wijnen, W., and Dochy, F., (1990), 'Performance Indicators: A New Management Technology for Higher Education? The Case of the United Kingdom, the Netherlands and Australia', in Dochy, F., et al (eds.), *Management Information and Performance Indicators in Higher Education: An International Issue*, Van Gorcum.

Selmes, C., (1989), 'Evaluation of Teaching', *Assessment and Evaluation in Higher Education*, Vol. 14, No. 3, Autumn, 167-178.

Sheppard, R., Last, R., and Foulkes, P., (1986), *The UGC Research Evaluations: Some Observations on Their Methodology and Results with Particular Reference to Departments of German*, Published by the authors.

Sher, I., and Garfield, E., (1966), 'New Tools for Improving and Evaluating the Effectiveness of Research', in Yovits, M. C., et al (eds.), *Research Program Effectiveness*, Gordon and Breach, New York.

Sizer, J., (1979), 'Assessing Institutional Performance: An Overview', *International Journal of Institutional Management in Higher Education*, Vol. 3, No. 1, 49-77.

Sizer, J., (1981), 'Performance Assessment in Institutions of Higher Education Under Conditions of Financial Stringency, Contraction and Changing Needs: A Management Accounting Perspective', *Accounting and Business Research*, Vol. 11, No. 43, 227-242.

Sizer, J., (1982), 'Assessing Institutional Performance and Progress' in Leslie Wagner (ed.), *Agenda for Institutional Change in Higher Education*, Society for Research in Higher Education, Monograph 45, 33-69.

Sizer, J., (1989), *Performance Indicators and Quality Control in Higher Education*, Keynote Address to an International Conference, Institute of Education, London.

Sizer, J., (1990), 'Performance Indicators and the Management of Universities in the UK: A Summary of Developments with Commentary', in Dochy, F., et al, (eds.) *Management Information and Performance Indicators in Higher Education: An International Issue*, Van Gorcum.

Sizer, J., and Frost, R., (1985), *Criteria for Self Evaluation of Department Research Profiles. Responsible and Responsive Universities Research Project*, Working Paper, Loughborough University of Technology. (Mimeo.)

Smith, R., and Fiedler, F., (1971), 'The Measurement of Scholarly Work: A Critical Review of the Literature', *Educational Record*, Summer, 225-232.

Smith, T., (1987), The UGC's Research Ranking Exercise, *Higher Education Quarterly*, Vol. 41, Autumn 1987, 303-316.

Smyth, F., and Anderson, J., (1987), *University Performance Indicators*, Science Policy Support Group Aide-Memoire No. 1, SPSG, London.

Solmon, L., and Astin, A., (1981), 'Departments Without Distinguished Graduate Programs', *Change*, Vol. 13, September, 23-28.

Spee, A., (ed.), (1990), *Development of Performance Indicators and Quality Assessment in Higher Education in the Netherlands*, Position Statement Prepared for the Meeting of the IMHE Project Group on the Development of Performance Indicators in Higher Education, Danburry Park, UK, 23-26 January.

STEAC Report, (1985), *Report of the Scottish Tertiary Education Advisory Council. Future Strategy for Higher Education in Scotland*, Cmnd 9676.

Sub Committee on Research Indicators (SCRI), (1989), *Issues in Quantitative Assessment of Departmental Research*, CVCP/UFC Performance Indicators Steering Company.

Sutherland Report, (1989), *The Teaching Function. Quality Assurance*, Committee of Vice-Chancellors and Principals, VC/89/160a.

Swinnerton-Dyer, Peter, (1986), Statement Made at the Higher Education Works for Schools Conference, Royal Institution, 24.11.86.

Talbot, R. W., and Bordage, G., (1986), 'A Preliminary Assessment of a New Method of Course Evaluation Based on Directed Small Group Discussions', *International Journal of Institutional Management in Higher Education*, Vol. 10, No. 2, July.

Taylor, J., (1985), *Comparing Universities: Some Observations on the First Destinations of New Graduates*, University of Lancaster, Discussion Paper, 85/11.

Taylor, T., (1985), 'A Value Added Student Assessment Model: Northeast Missouri State University', *Assessment and Evaluation in Higher Education*, Vol. 10, No. 3, 190-202.

Taylor, M., (1989), 'Recent Changes in National Higher Education Policies', *Higher Education Management*, Vol. 1, No. 3, 314-322.

Taylor, M., (1989a), 'The Implications of New Organisational Patterns of Research, *Higher Education Management*, Vol. 1, No. 1, March, 7-19.

Taylor, J., and Johnes, J., (1989), 'An Evaluation of Performance Indicators Based Upon the First Destination of University Graduates, *Studies in Higher Education*, Vol. 14, No. 2, 201-217.

Teichler, V., (1988), *Changing Patterns of the Higher Education System: The Experience of Three Decades*, Jessica Kingsley.

Tomkins, C., and Green, R., (1988), 'An Experiment in the Use of Data Envelopment Analysis for Evaluating the Efficiency of UK University Departments of Accounting', *Financial Accountability and Management*.

Torode, P., (1980), 'Course Review at Newcastle upon Tyne Polytechnic', in Billing, D., (ed.), *Indicators of Performance*, The Society for Research into Higher Education.

Treasury, (1987), *The Government's Expenditure Plans, 1987-8 to 1989-90*, (Public Expenditure White Paper), Cm 56, HMSO.

Trow, M., (1986), *Academic Standards and Mass Higher Education*, Paper Prepared for the Conference on Quality Assurance in First Degree Courses, Sponsored by Higher Education International, 1986.

Universities Funding Council, (1989), Circular Letter 27/89, *Research Selectivity Exercise 1989. The Outcome.*

Universities Funding Council, (1989), Circular Letter 39/89, *Funding and Planning:1991/92 to 1994/95.*

Universities Funding Council, (1989) *Report on the 1989 Research Assessment Exercise.*

Universities Funding Council, (1990), Circular Letter 29/90, *Funding and Planning Exercise.*

University Grants Committee, (1984), Circular Letter 17/84, *Planning for the Late 1980s.*

University Grants Committee, (1984), *A Strategy for Higher Education into the 1990s.*

University Grants Committee, (1985), Circular 12/85, *Planning for the Late 1980s.*

University Grants Committee, (1985), Circular Letter 22/85, *Planning for the Late 1980s: The Resource Allocation Process.*

University Grants Committee, (1986), Circular Letter 4/86, *Planning for the Late 1980s: Recurrent Grant for 1986/7.*

University Grants Committee, (1988), Circular Letter 15/88, *The Next Research Selectivity Exercise: Consultative Paper.*

University Grants Committee, (1988), Circular Letter 45/88, *Research Selectivity Exercise, 1989.*

Van Vught, F., (1988), 'A New Autonomy in European Higher Education? An Explanation and Analysis of the Strategy of Self-Regulation in Higher Education', *International Journal of Institutional Management in Higher Education*, Vol. 12, 16-26.

Warnock Report, (1990), *Teaching Quality: Report of the Committee of Enquiry Appointed by the Council*, PCFC.

Webster, D., (1981), 'Advantages and Disadvantages of Methods of Assessing Quality', *Change*, Vol. 13, October 1981, 20-24.

Winter Hebron, C. de, (1984), 'An Aid for Evaluating Teaching in 'Higher Education', *Assessment and Evaluation in Higher Education*, Vol. 9, No. 2, Summer, 145-163.

Wright, G., (1989), 'Draft Report of the Directorate Resources Network Steering Group on Performance Indicators, 1987', in Pratt, J., (ed.), *Report of a Conference on Performance Indicators in Teacher Education*, Centre for Institutional Studies, Polytechnic of East London.

Wright, J., (1987), 'A Big Stick Without a Carrot', *Times Higher Education Supplement*, 27.2.87, 14.

Zander, M., (1986), Letter to *The Times*, 11.7.86.

Ziman, J., (1987), *Science in a Steady State: The Research System in Transition*, Science Policy Support Group, London.

Ziman, J., (1989) *Restructuring Academic Science: A New Framework for UK Policy*, Science Policy Support Group, London.

Index